About the Author

Dr. Richard Benton earned his MA and PhD in Hebrew and Semitic Studies from the University of Wisconsin-Madison, and MDiv from St. Vladimir's Orthodox Theological Seminary, Crestwood, New York. He has taught in the areas of Jewish Studies, Biblical Studies, Biblical Hebrew, and Comparative Monotheisms at the University of Balamand, El-Khoura, Lebanon, the Ukrainian Catholic University, Lviv, Ukraine, as well as universities in Wisconsin and Washington State. Along with Fr. Marc Boulos, he co-hosts *The Bible as Literature* podcast, which examines how the narrative, literary arc of the Bible functions for its readers.

Praise for *Hosea*

"Crisply written, a boon to all students of the prophet Hosea."

John Hobbins, PhD
Trinity Lutheran Seminary, Gambela, Ethiopia
Pastor, Zion Lutheran Church
Oshkosh WI

"As an ordained pastor of forty-eight years I was always looking for ways to preach from both scripture and the newspaper as Dr. Karl Barth advised a hundred years ago. Dr. Benton has provided a current interpretation of Hosea that helps to resource such a goal. This is so helpful in times of untruth, injustice and growing economic inequality. And the translation of the Hebrew was alive with meaning as a picture language should be."

Pastor Donald G. Marxhausen
Evangelical Lutheran Church of America
Highland's Ranch, Colorado

"In his marvelously clear translation of — and commentary on — the book of Hosea, Richard Benton displays his own prophetic voice. That is, he reanimates not only Hosea, the first of twelve "minor" prophets in the Tanakh, but also the eleven others by showing how they're connected and how their consistent message resounds today. Hosea's life-giving words may have been written for residents of the northern kingdom of Israel in the Eighth Century BCE, but Benton has resurrected them so they speak this simple message directly to us in the Twenty-first Century: Trust in God and be kind."

Bill Tammeus
Former Faith section columnist, *The Kansas City Star*
Author, *The Value of Doubt: Why Unanswered Questions, Not Unquestioned Answers, Build Faith.*

"For laity who may struggle with the relevance of Hosea's message against idolatry, Benton brings thoughtful theological insights which are both challenging and very much applicable to faith and life today. For teachers and pastors who may shy away from Hosea's dense and difficult poetic language, he provides uncommon clarity without losing sight of the details that matter."

Kevin Chau, PhD
University of the Free State
Bloemfontein, South Africa

"In his commentary on Hosea, Dr. Richard Benton transports the hearer across space and time, continent and century, to guide them through a tour of the common and timeless human tools of abuse uncovered by scripture. When we get early access to resources, we horde them, and commit violence to maintain the status quo. When we feel insecure, we scapegoat the stranger in our midst."

Deacon Henok Elias
Virgin Mary's Ethiopian Orthodox Tewahido Cathedral
Los Angeles, California

"Benton's masterful elucidation of the text of Hosea reveals the prophetic timelessness of its diagnosis of the fundamental human predicament, namely "forgetting" Yhwh in knowledge, trust, and obedience (cf. Deut 8:11-20). Arising out of natural human fear and security, this abandonment of trust in Yhwh's sovereignty--along with all the providence and protection a divine patron would be in a position to offer--leads human beings to seek control of the flow of goods for themselves or, in Hosea's terms, seeking other lovers. Benton's argument compels the reader to consider how such misplaced trust in institutions of political and religious "leadership"—and more importantly in one's own Self—may be considered an insidious form of idolatry and therefore an illusory bulwark against disaster, as eighth-century BCE Israel experienced for itself. Standing alongside the book of Hosea, Benton's commentary compels us to consider an ultimate question, "Who are our baals?""

Nicolae Roddy, PhD
Professor of Hebrew Bible, Creighton University
Omaha, Nebraska

The Book of the Twelve: A Commentary

Volume 1: Hosea

THE CHRYSOSTOM BIBLE
A Commentary Series for Preaching and Teaching

In the Series

Genesis

Philippians

Romans

Colossians & Philemon

1 Corinthians

Ezekiel

Joshua

2 Corinthians

Isaiah

Jeremiah

Hebrews

The Pastorals

Ephesians & 2 Thessalonians

THE CHRYSOSTOM BIBLE
A Commentary Series for Preaching and Teaching

The Book of the Twelve: A Commentary

Volume 1: Hosea

Richard Benton

OCABS PRESS
ST PAUL, MINNESOTA 55124
2021

The Book of the Twelve: A Commentary
Volume 1: Hosea

Copyright © 2021 by Richard Benton
All rights reserved.

ISBN 1-60191-051-7

Published by OCABS Press, St. Paul, Minnesota.
Printed in the United States of America.

Books are available through OCABS Press at special discounts for bulk purchases in the United States by academic institutions, churches, and other organizations. For more information please email OCABS Press at press@ocabs.org.

To Hollie

*Give to her from the fruit of her hands,
and her works will praise her in the gates.
(Prov 31:31)*

Contents

Preface	xiii
Acknowledgments	xvii
Introduction	1
Chapter 1	37
Chapter 2	51
Chapter 3	73
Chapter 4	81
Chapter 5	99
Chapter 6	119
Chapter 7	131
Chapter 8	145
Chapter 9	159
Chapter 10	173
Chapter 11	191
Chapter 12	205
Chapter 13	221
Chapter 14	235
Conclusions	245

Preface

The present Bible Commentary Series is not so much in honor of John Chrysostom as it is to continue and promote his legacy as an interpreter of the biblical texts for preaching and teaching God's congregation, in order to prod its members to proceed on the way they started when they accepted God's calling. Chrysostom's virtual uniqueness is that he did not subscribe to any hermeneutic or methodology, since this would amount to introducing an extra-textual authority over the biblical texts. For him, scripture is its own interpreter. Listening to the texts time and again allowed him to realize that "call" and "read (aloud)" are not interconnected realities; rather, they are one reality since they both are renditions of the same Hebrew verb *qara'*. Given that words read aloud are words of instruction for one "to do them," the only valid reaction would be to hear, listen, obey, and abide by these words. All these connotations are subsumed in the same Hebrew verb *šama'*. On the other hand, these scriptural "words of life" are presented as readily understandable utterances of a father to his children (Isaiah 1:2-3). The recipients are never asked to engage in an intellectual debate with their divine instructor, or even among themselves, to fathom what he is saying. The Apostle to the Gentiles followed in the footsteps of the Prophets to Israel by handing down to them the Gospel, that is, the Law of God's Spirit through his Christ (Romans 8:2; Galatians 6:2) as fatherly instruction (1 Corinthians 4:15). He in turn wrote readily understandable letters to be read aloud. It is in these same footsteps that Chrysostom followed, having learned from both the Prophets and Paul that the same "words of life" carry also the sentence of death at the hand of the scriptural God, Judge of all (Deuteronomy 28; Joshua 8:32-35; Psalm 82; Matthew 3:4-12; Romans 2:12-16; 1 Corinthians 10:1-11; Revelation 20:11-15).

While theological debates and hermeneutical theories come and go after having fed their proponents and their fans with passing human glory, the Golden Mouth's expository homilies, through the centuries, fed and still feed myriads of believers in so many traditions and countries. Virtually banned from dogmatic treatises, he survives in the hearts of "those who have ears to hear." His success is due to his commitment to exegesis rather than to futile hermeneutics. The latter behaves as someone who dictates on a living organism what it is supposed to be, whereas exegesis submits to that organism and endeavors to decipher it through trial and error. There is as much a far cry between the text and the theories about it as there is between a living organism and the theories about it. The biblical texts are the reality of God imparted through their being read aloud in the midst of the congregation, disregarding the value of the sermon that follows. The sermon, much less a theological treatise, is at best an invitation to hear and obey the text. Assessing the shape of an invitation card has no value whatsoever when it comes to the dinner itself; the guests are fed by the dinner, not by the invitation or its phrasing (Luke 14:16-24; Matthew 22:1-14).

This commentary series does not intend to promote Chrysostom's ideas as a public relation manager would do, but rather to follow in the footsteps of his approach as true children and heirs are expected to do. He used all the contemporary tools at his disposal to communicate God's written instruction to his hearers, as a doctor would with his patients, without spending unnecessary energy on peripheral debates requiring the use of professional jargon incomprehensible to the commoner. The writers of this series will try to do the same: muster to the best of their ability all necessary contemporary knowledge to communicate to the general readers the biblical message without burdening them with data unnecessary for that purpose. Whenever it will be deemed necessary or even helpful to do so, and in order to curtail burdensome and lengthy technical asides within the commentaries, specialized monographs related either to specific topics or to the scriptural background—literary, socio-political, or archeological—will be issued as companions to the series.

Paul Nadim Tarazi
Editor

Acknowledgments

I would like to dedicate this work to my first teacher in the Scriptures, the Very Reverend Dr. Paul Nadim Tarazi, who toiled to plant this seed in my life. He taught the first courses that I took in the Bible at St. Vladimir's Seminary and directed my M.Div. thesis in harlotry in the Hebrew Bible, where this work began. His shocking use of the Bible to direct our thinking towards self-analysis and -criticism opened a world of personal and academic labor that is only beginning to bear fruit in me. He has spent countless hours working with me to the present—including many drafts of this present work—and surely more hours thinking about my work than I deserve.

I would also like to express my gratitude to my doctoral professors, first my *Doktormutter,* Prof. Cynthia Miller-Naudé, who not only taught me the painstaking skills for linguistic and literary analysis, but also the value of meticulous copyediting. Without her many hours of work in teaching me, I would not be able to reach the depths that I have found. Second, Prof. Michael Fox taught me that the language of the Bible runs infinitely deep. From him I learned not even to trust the dictionary, but only the usage of language that we find in the text itself.

The constant presence of my friend and co-laborer, the Very Reverend Fr. Marc Boulos, pressed me onwards in work when other forces pulled me away. Not one to be able to look at a project unfinished, he never ceased in his encouragement to continue in this study of Hosea.

Finally, my deepest gratitude extends to my wife, Hollie. Even when it meant the continuous disparity of housework, she encouraged me to continue on writing this book. Her dedicated labor to our family and to the work that I was producing allowed me the effort that this book represents. I cannot thank her enough for providing that space in my—our—life for this book to exist.

May this work be faithful to their labor.

Richard Benton

Introduction

*Y*ou abandoned Yhwh, your god. You followed after other gods as if they were your father, just as your whore of a mother looked for other men. You denied the faithfulness of Yhwh within hours of declaring your trust.

As soon as you looked to the sky for rain, as soon as you lifted a stone for your protective walls, you rejected Yhwh. You called your desire for safety "practicality," and then turned from your god. As soon as your warehouses and bank accounts were full, you congratulated yourself—and yourself alone.

Yhwh required truth and mercy from you, and you obeyed him—only in your own way. You murdered your brother and called it "truth." You ignored the poor and called it "mercy."

Your priests served the Baals faithfully. They gave you calves to kiss when you murdered your brother and when the fields were dry and when your enemies attacked your gates. When you sinned, they gladly accepted rich offerings for your atonement. They might have shaken their heads when you sinned, but they promised you would be forgiven at the right price. But they never taught you how—or why—to stop sinning.

You had one job to do: prove to Yhwh that you were his son. Your mother spent her life with different men. You just needed to recognize Yhwh and follow his instruction, his Torah, to show that nine months before your birth it was Yhwh whom your mom happened to be sleeping with.

I gave birth to you in Egypt so you could be my son. I gave you Torah for wisdom and life. I sustained you in a wilderness that otherwise could not give life. Yet you looked for Baals. I will give *birth again, but this time from Assyria. I will offer Torah again, but this time to your children.*

Will they accept it?

Origins of Israel's whoring

"Go, take for yourself a woman of whoring and children of whoring," Yhwh began in the Book of Hosea. In the beginning, the land was a whore, and her children—the people—had no clear father.

Yhwh spoke to Moses at Sinai with a commandment of hope,

> I am the Lord your God, who brought you out of the land of Egypt, out of the house of bondage. There shall not be for you other gods before me.[1]

Israel had one god, who was more powerful than their oppressor, Pharaoh.

The two passages offered a stark choice: a single god without peer or whoredom. Before Yhwh led them into the land, he gave them a choice: unequivocal submission to his teaching or rebellion. If they chose to follow idols, they would be taken out of the land, into a land to serve idols, but if they sought Yhwh, they would not destroy them.[2] The one who would ensure their prosperity is Yhwh, the one who brought them out of Egypt.[3] The prosperity, however, could be their downfall, as they could forget that Yhwh brought them out of Egypt and kept them alive in the

---

[1] Exod 20:3-4.

[2] Deut 4:25-31.

[3] Deut 6:10-15.

Introduction

desert. Alternatively, they might presume that they kept themselves alive then and caused their own prosperity today.[4]

The great sin imagined in Deuteronomy, therefore, is self-reliance. In their imagination, Israel's sons freed themselves and kept themselves free. They prospered because of their own hands. They held power that needed no being to bring them out of Egypt, and that retained no fear of one who could send them back.

These passages from Deuteronomy forge an ironclad link between self-reliance and idolatry. Chapter 4 alternates between a פסל, *pesel*, "graven image," that they make for themselves and the מעשה ידי אדם, *ma'asê yadey 'adam*, "the work of a person's hands," whom they will serve in captivity. Idols, by definition, are gods that humans create. Should the people forget Yhwh, the origin of the prosperity in the land in ch. 6, they will turn to other gods, begetting sources of prosperity entirely under their control.

The land committed its original sin, as we see in Hos 1, when it sought good fortune from Baals instead of Yhwh. She wanted her lover, Baal, to provide for her, not her husband. With her beauty, she tried to seduce him, never realizing that Yhwh provided the beauty she used on her lovers.

Baals promised security. Yhwh's wife, the land, claimed that they were "the givers of my bread and my water, my wool and my flax, my oil and my drink" (2:7). They gave, and they did not take away. The land wanted assurance, that she would have everything she wanted, not matter what.

Yhwh controlled everything, however. The truth was, "she did not know that [Yhwh] gave her the grain and the new wine and

---

[4] Deut 8:11-17.

the oil" (2:10). The security that the Baals promised was a lie, and the truth was that prosperity came with the expectation of loyalty. At the same time, Yhwh could take it all away. If she did not return to him he would "strip her naked and establish her like the day of her birth," "set her like a dry land," and "kill her with thirst" (2:5).

The people of Israel, the daughters of the land, were supposed to be Yhwh's children, but the dalliances of the land raised the question: was their father Yhwh, or one of their mother's lovers? Yhwh desired for the people to be his children, but he could not tell. They would have to show their loyalty by obeying him. They had to choose: either hear his word and follow it or follow their own hearts that inspired the idolatrous work of their hands.

Fear causing oppression

Those who establish rules in society tend to be those who hold the most resources and who fear losing what they have. Hence, they do not predicate regulation on fair distribution and risk their reservoir, but concentrate on increasing the flow. Fear motivates evil as well as the human solutions for evil.

Evil begins with forgetting Yhwh's salvation in Egypt, which leaves humans anxious. Finding oneself in an insecure position, one has no reason to trust that Yhwh will deliver from destruction, let alone discomfort. This dread leads one to "do something," and that "deed" initiates idolatry. In our modern society, we manifest that self-reliance in imaginative and grandiose ways. Fear at once presses us towards building up civilization, an idolatrous mechanism to create and preserve prosperity, and away from Yhwh, the source of prosperity.

Throughout human history, people lived at a subsistence level. They gathered, hunted, or farmed, and had just about enough to

Introduction 5

survive—sometimes more, sometimes less. If we imagine prosperity as a stream, at times nature provided a torrent of good things for humans to live on, while at others, only a trickle.

Rather than submit to the ebbs and flows of nature, fear spurs humans to regulate the stream of prosperity. We save and hoard during prosperous times to balance out the lean times we fear. We put in a dam that stops the flow to create a reservoir for our private use. Those downstream then receive less. Their fear increased, they build their own dams. The stream no longer flows, but fills people's personal reservoirs.

The greediest and most cautious end up richest, while those who trust in abundance look foolish. Imagine a corporation that paid all its employees according to how much each wanted to take—no paychecks, but a common ATM for everyone to withdraw from. Some would greedily amass money for things they *did not* need, like a cruise or a third television. Others would cautiously take for things they *might* need, like a sick relative who might get worse. A few would frugally withdraw *precisely* what they needed. If the ATM stopped dispensing, the greediest would be in the best shape and those who took the least would perish.

The best solution that the powerful could come up with would be to regulate greed, to be sure that distribution occurred "fairly." To introduce "fairness," one may suggest rules to determine who needs how much, and a bureaucracy to carry it out. Money for a sick relative is a "need," while money for a relative who might hypothetically get sick is not. Money for a relative is a "need," but not money for a dear friend. Cancer would constitute "sick," but not the flu. Those who work harder or hold more important positions would get more. The same ones to invent these rules would, naturally, also adjudicate these situations.

Institutions of fear: Government and religion

Creation of government to control

> There is no king saved by multitude of might; a mighty man is not delivered by multitude of strength. The horse is deceit for salvation, and by the multitude of his might he will not help escape (Ps 33:16-17).

The rules that humans create for distribution crystalize into bureaucracies, which morph into militarized governments. They gather and distribute resources, provide common services, and defend themselves with force. In other words, they control the wealth of the people and the force to maintain control. Ideally, they distribute to all freely, but in reality, those in control never go hungry even in the worst of times.

Aristocracies and oligarchies emerge, and rather than stream wealth from one group to another, they dam the flow. At that nexus of control, individuals constantly choose between generosity and greed, holding in their hand the means to alleviate the gap between the rich and the poor. At the hint of fear, though, those in power inevitably perpetuate the division. They ensure the existence of their pools, even if they have to reduce the flow downstream to zero.

The powerful construct a reality that perpetuates their prosperity. A government may decide to entomb Pharaoh in a pyramid to perpetuate the king's position into the afterlife. Another government may decide on an interstate highway system to ensure commerce and domestic defense. A massive pool of resources is used to keep that same pool full.

As they see projects they want done, whether pyramids or interstates, they bring in the poor to perform their tasks. They may enslave people to work or offer them a job with wages, but they will let as little through the "dam" as possible to complete the project. They pay workers based on the perceived value of the tasks they perform. Those in power allow access to wealth as an incentive to coerce the poor to act in a particular way, not as a means for having what they need. The promise of more wealth drives the system, not a desire to cover needs.

The military victimizes the outsider

In order to regulate the economy, governments require a military to react to fear of shortages and fear of attack. They first claim their "reservoir," the resources that belong to them, which determines who they will allow to receive. A surplus can result in attacks when outsiders desire the bounty, and a shortage may require taking the resources of others. Force is required in both scenarios.

Deciding who has and does not have the right to drink from the reservoir establishes insiders and outsiders. With respect to governments, the distinction is a legal one. The first duty is toward insiders, or fellow citizens. A government may establish different sets of rules for citizens and non-citizens. Citizens of the US, for example, are allowed to receive Medicare and Social Security; illegal immigrants are not.

At a sign of hostility from foreigner against citizen, a government engages its military. Such hostility may take the form of foreign aggression against citizens, or of foreigners hoarding resources needed by citizens. A military will protect the health and security of its citizens even at the expense of foreign lives. The military is ready to kill an outsider who would wish to harm them or withhold needed resources.

These institutions ostensibly exist to protect citizens, but they also take advantage of insider/outsider distinctions inside the country, even inflicting violence domestically. Punishment can be directed at particular communities on legal grounds for the sake of continuing stability for the government's institutions. For example, a government can crack down on one distinct group because of perceived foreignness, such as the US sending Americans of Japanese descent to inland concentration camps, or the Nazis murdering hundreds of thousands of Romany people. By taking advantage of such distinctions, a government skews punishment and rule of law against this "outsider" from among the country's insiders to sustain its own power.

Militaries place the weakest citizens in harm's way as they ostensibly fight to protect citizens. Governments fill the military with the rich and powerful to make decisions, and with poor citizens to commit the acts of violence—often against equally powerless foreigners. In feudal Europe, soldiers came from among the farmers of a landowner to fight against those of another landowner. In the all-voluntary military of the modern US, soldiers come from the least powerful of society, whereas officers come from the highest. In modern Russia, where service is mandatory for all, those with social connections manage to avoid the worst, most dangerous jobs. In waging war, the rich build bunkers or conduct airlifts or bribe their way out of war zones, while the disenfranchised remain on the front lines without exit, exposed. The poor disproportionately bear the brunt of violence.[5]

---

[5] When the US went to war in Vietnam, for example, the majority of US soldiers on the front lines came from the lowest, least powerful ranks of society. Even though service was mandatory and selection was random, one could avoid danger. For example, those in college could defer. Those with connections could serve in the National Guard. With

Religion controls source of prosperity

Fear that prosperity might stop flowing also motivates humans' desire for religion. What if threats to prosperity come from natural sources and not human ones? What if a flood wipes out an agricultural or manufacturing center? What if a disease hits one's crops, or if markets crash? At the very head of the stream of prosperity sits a power. When we anthropomorphize the power of the source, we create a god. Fertility gods appear abundantly in many cultures. For example, archaeologists have found thousands of clay figurines from Iron Age Judah that depict a female torso of robust proportions, symbolizing fecundity.[6] Elsewhere, such powers may be manifested as gods of the sky and the storm, or of the source of a stream, or of the buffalo, or as an all-encompassing deity. Religion steps in to help ensure or restore prosperity *supernaturally*.

Religions assume a limit to the amount of prosperity that the gods can or will provide, and so sets up a system of who should and should not receive prosperity. Humans seem naturally inclined to doubt the ability of the divine to provide for all. Just as governments separate citizen from foreigner, religions separate

---

money, one could find a doctor who could be influenced to discover a reason for the conscript not to serve. The poor were left over for the actual fighting.

Among the Vietnamese, many more poor civilians suffered than soldiers. As US forces fought through the countryside, they encountered villages of poor farmers. The Vietnamese military may have protected this or that village, as the military elite saw fit. Vietnamese soldiers who protected the civilians also came from these same villages. As poor soldier and poor civilian were difficult to distinguish, both suffered violence at the hands of US soldiers. They had poverty and lack of power in common. The poor US soldier confronted the poor Vietnamese farmer for the sake of objectives determined by the powerful in Paris, Washington, and Saigon.

[6] They are also known as "Judahite pillar figurines" or JPFs. See Robert Deutsch, "JPFs: More Questions than Answers," *Biblical Archaeological Review* 40, no. 5 (September/October 2014): 37-39.

true believers from unbelievers. Since experience shows that not everyone receives an equal amount of prosperity, believers ensure they are among those who receive even when the unbelievers go without.

Religion functions for people to remain in their god's good graces by offering a code of conduct from "on high" for adherents (insiders) to follow. Those who follow it will be "in" with the deity and will enjoy prosperity, and those who do not follow it will remain outside the group and the prosperity its members enjoy. Perhaps the code addresses our conduct, such as not stealing or lying. There might also be arbitrary actions for adherents to follow, such as wearing something on our head or gathering as a community weekly on such-and-such a day. We ensure we are correct and "good with God" and so control the flow of prosperity from him, linking our actions to the deity's moods, manipulating the power for ourselves.

Such external indicators distinguish insiders clearly, so we can ensure the exclusion of others who do not follow this code. Religious people assume that their god's ultimate wish is their fellow-insiders' safety and security, and that the deity stands with them against the outsider. Religious groups may publicize problems caused by another group toward their religion, or even make public their own invective against another religion, such as when Christian groups disparage Judaism or Islam. Whether one calls the outsider an "unbeliever," a "foreigner," or a "non-citizen," we rally the insider to keep us safe from the outsider and protect our prosperity. We pray our god will prevent any phenomenon that might harm us.

As our god is stronger than we are and cannot be controlled by force, humans attempt to control it by coercion. Through prayer, one petitions the deity for prosperity and wealth. Sacrifice to the deity substantiates our willingness to give up those valued things we ask for, like grain or money. Blood sacrifice further intensifies prayer through death and spilling blood. Preparing a feast or an offering to the poor imitates the generosity we hope the deity will carry out for us. At times, the god of prosperity may be holding back what we want because he seems angry, so we show how sorry we are by performing rites of mourning, as if someone died. We impose self-affliction for the sake of the god. Fasting or wearing certain mournful clothing can fill this role.

With so many available methods of influencing a deity, people want to know the most effective one for a given situation, so they need to discern the divine mood and intent. Someone may have offended and angered a god through an action, for example. If the god felt angry, he might cause a drought. Therefore, one invents divination to read and understand the will of the god(s) to determine the next actions for humans to take to ensure prosperity. Divination assumes that gods communicate through natural phenomena when they are angry, so if one divines this anger, one can convince them through the above means not to cause the drought. Diviners thus read aspects of the natural world, such as sheep livers, bird flights, astronomical phenomena, or tea leaves, which correlate with other natural phenomena caused by heavenly beings. Thus, the people, armed with skillful diviners, can keep themselves safe.

The story of Cain and Abel describes the madness that resulted from one man's inability to influence the deity through sacrifice. Cain's sacrifice of the fruits of the earth did not garner him the favor that Abel's sacrifice of animal flesh did. Bounty depends on Yhwh's favor, and Cain was upset—maybe worried—that Yhwh did not favor him. Even though the narrative describes no implications about receiving Yhwh's material favor or not, Cain could not stand it (Gen 4:5).

Our father, Cain, invented the first dam of prosperity. Abel was a shepherd, and so spent his time outside in search of bounty and prosperity for his flocks. Cain, in contrast, was a farmer, who worked the same fields daily (Gen 4:2). One difference between livestock and crops is that the latter can be stored for lean years. Logically, Cain founded the first city (Gen 4:17) to store grain and protect it from animals and humans who would eat it. Abel's livestock, in contrast, is much more vulnerable to both. Cain manifests the human longing for security, depending on our invention and foresight to protect ourselves. Abel, the shepherd, depended on Yhwh for safety and comfort. The city Cain invented ensured that humans would no longer depend on the vicissitudes of nature. Its storehouses kept him safe from famine, and its walls, safe from foreigners. Moreover, Cain is the father of jealousy, concerned about Yhwh's favor. Cain, therefore, manifests the fear of losing favor with his god and of lacking prosperity.

Cain's jealousy is further manifested in the religious distinction between insider and outsider. He could not stand to be an outsider, while Abel was an insider who took on as a shepherd the constant risk to his prosperity. Cain performed the right cultic action, but was not favored, and it drove him mad. As religious people, we reject Yhwh's ability to show bounty to all by demanding that he favor us more than "them" because we are so desperate for his favor to ensure our future bounty. The insider/outsider distinction manifests our father Cain's jealousy

Introduction

that Yhwh might favor our brother and not provide us with prosperity.[7]

The Origin of Science

Much of science flows from the same source as religious thinking: the desire to ensure prosperity. Religious thinking hopes to manipulate prosperity by supernatural means. Science arises from this same hope, but by natural means.

We can observe an early form of the scientific method in the divination of the ancient Babylonians. Lest we assume that divination arose entirely from the active imaginations of the ancients, we should note that they followed a clear method: they listed a phenomenon, predictions about the related phenomenon (hypothesis), and the actual outcome. For example, they observed a particular alignment of heavenly bodies, predicted a drought, and then recorded whether a drought in fact came. If outcomes did not align with predictions, they could alter their interpretation of the same phenomenon in the future to align with the previously observed result. For example, if a drought did not come as

---

[7] Forms of worship need not be limited to manipulation of material prosperity, for devotion to the gods can come from bona fide feelings of love and respect toward the divine being. Instead of a flow of material prosperity, though, we try to influence the flow of good feelings within ourselves. Human beings across cultures feel a connection with the "numinous," which seems to come and go arbitrarily, and it can lead to feelings of mystical connections to the divine. For such people, connecting with the divine functions as a source of prosperity, as well. As a result, this feeling is subject to human attempts at manipulation. While these feelings normally come on their own, humans try to evoke them by actions such as meditation, self-flagellation, dance, or repetition of sounds. Once one seeks to invoke feelings of or contact with the numinous, one is coercing the deity; hence the above paradigm still applies. The religious actions change our natural state to actively bring the emotion back, as if our natural state is blocking it. We must change the state of (our) nature—or ask our deity to do so—for the good feelings to flow, because we are impatient that the good feelings may not return soon enough.

predicted, they could correct their astrological model. In this way, they sought to improve their ability to discern and predict significant natural phenomena through consistent interpretation of the gods' intentions.[8] Their lists correlated phenomena, which they sought to generalize as indicative.

Modern science resembles Babylonian divination. Genetic engineering, for example, includes the same motivation to control prosperity in its pursuit of better health or greater agricultural yields. The scientist connects and correlates natural phenomena to arrive at the source of the phenomenon under investigation. The religious mind assumes that the chain of causation leads back to an anthropomorphic mind and appeals directly to it; the scientist simply moves back in the chain one step at a time, with less concern for the primary cause. The religious person wants to influence Aristotle's Unmoved Mover; the scientist seeks to understand the movements and influence them. The pursuits of much of modern science reinforce that human beings of every stripe, religious or atheist, fear the loss of prosperity.

The scientific Babylonian soothsayer and the modern geneticist both seek answers to the same question: how do we ensure bounty? But this question betrays the underlying assumption: there might not be enough.

Creating and caring for the poor

We trust only our dams, refusing to trust that enough will come our way. We would rather live exclusively off what we have pooled up for ourselves. But it is only the work of our own hands that

---

[8] Francesca Rochberg, "Empiricism in Babylonian Omen Texts and the Classification of Mesopotamian Divination as Science," *Journal of the American Oriental Society* 119, no. 4 (Oct. - Dec., 1999): 559-69.

Introduction 15

performs the divine function, to provide the reassurance that we are desperate for.

The sickness of fear causes societal symptoms. Just as there are different types of cancer—lung, colon, brain, etc.—fear manifests itself in different places in different ways, such as science, religion, charitable organizations, or politics. Moreover, these institutions, like cancer, sap an inordinate amount of energy from the rest of the body, until the body cannot be sustained. Fear dams prosperity, taking more than needed, like cancer takes more blood and nutrients. No methods to help or feed the poor address the true cause of poverty: our greed, born of insecurity and lack of trust.

No matter how much we try to manipulate the cosmos through the gods made by our hands, we are stuck with our underlying willfulness and fear that come from our lack of faith. Even religious, scientific, and government experts who successfully bring more prosperity to others, as long as they continue to dam up prosperity for themselves, betray their pathological fear of dependence on nature to provide for them. Ironically, the dams our fear builds perpetuate the poverty we convince ourselves that we are reducing.

When we recognize how much richer we are than others, many of us struggle with guilt, which prompts us to seize agency to remove this bad feeling. "How can we help those less fortunate than ourselves?" we muse. In this way, we significantly change the initial question from, "How do I trust the natural flow of prosperity?" to "How do I increase others' prosperity (without giving up any of my own)?" As gods of our own making, we invent different means to help. Whatever means we—through our gods—employ to increase the amount of food and reduce hunger, we want a say in the outcome to preserve ourselves.

Feeding the poor is not the matter, but the human self-righteous lack of trust that created the poverty in the first place. Rather than give up what they already have, the geneticist justifies herself, "I can feed more people this way," and the suburban Christian justifies himself, "I pray that God will take care of them." We want the poor fed, but we do not want to give up our unfair share, so creating programs and praying for them help us feel justified. Our actions prove that we do not trust that free-flowing prosperity would offer us enough, otherwise we would be willing to give up what we have. At the same time, we persuade the poor to trust in our programs and our prayers. Let us not think that "the poor" are virtuously exempt from this thinking: they desire to build their own dams so that they can count on themselves, rather than what comes to them from "the rich."

Our system of "caring for" the poor is based on faulty assumptions, namely, we have to fix "the poor" rather than fixing ourselves. We want to make a difference in the world, unaware of the moral imperative we have for our own sake. Our work, we idealize, will add to the stream of prosperity, which will trickle down to the poor. We presume that taking care of the poor means to fix "them" and their state, not "us." Wealthy donors want to fix education in poor inner-city neighborhoods, and so use their money to start up expensive programs in those schools. They do not work towards breaking down the tax system that keeps their copious tax dollars in their own school system, where their privileged sons and daughters study.

Control directs our sense of mercy. We do not immediately offer food when the hungry confront us. A homeless person is turned

Introduction 17

away from a restaurant, even though the establishment throws away pounds of food daily. A grocery store will give generously to "community programs," but locks its dumpsters at night. When we confront the naked, we do not simply offer a coat. When we confront the poor, we do not give money. Instead, we create mechanisms and institutions between us and them. When we choose to help, we create welfare states and food banks, and we donate unwanted clothes to professional donors.

Geneticists get rich inventing ways to feed the poor with more resources. How do they justify themselves? They feed more people with less, but at what cost? Scientists create cheaper crops that require fewer resources to grow, which seems like a boon. Cheaper and more abundant food! Among other advantages, McDonald's restaurants benefit by being able to sell cheaper burgers. After making cheeseburgers all day long, McDonald's throws any leftovers in the trash rather than give them to the needy. While more poor people are able to live off hamburgers, their health deteriorates. Rural areas become awash in enormous factory farms of corn and soy, so that the workers on the farm cannot afford vegetables—which have to be shipped in from hundreds of miles away. The seeds are then patented, to enrich the inventors, marketers, and distributors. Yet once the seeds are patented, the farmers go further into debt.

How many millions of dollars are spent on genetic engineering instead of feeding the poor? Ultimately, genetic advances enrich McDonald's, factory farms, and genetic modification firms, while the wealth, health, and well-being of many needy people decline. Such are the results when these scientists address the incorrect question of how to feed the poor, and ignore the correct one: how to eliminate their personal fear of giving up what they have. It is easier for them to engineer new crops than change their eating habits.

How does the suburban Christian justify himself? "I pray that God will provide as I donate to groups dedicated to helping the poor." How can he live in a suburban neighborhood, separated from the poor, with thousands of dollars in the bank, and ask God to provide? He could have sold his expensive house, bought a cheap house in the inner city, and given the difference to his poor neighbors. Why turn over the duty to provide to others when he has distanced himself from those in need? By living in the suburbs, he chose to remove himself from the urban reality of his actions. He removed any responsibility to reform himself and asks God to take over his responsibility.

Ironically, "charitable" organizations require resources to exist, resources that otherwise could have gone to the poor. I can set up a trust and invest a million dollars to give $10,000 to the needy every year. I count on the economy to help the poor, with my seed money. My job is quickly done. "Investment," though, does not happen on its own; money is given to *companies* for them to prosper. But what companies does that money go to? What role do they have in creating poverty? The original million served the rich in whom one invested; it never helped the poor. Only the "extra" money that the companies offered in dividends helped those in need. What if the economy crashes? Then the million and the $10,000 will disappear, benefitting no one.

Furthermore, we assume that we through our institutions have unlimited time. Nothing guarantees that our investments to help the poor "down the road" will help anyone, or that the institutions we set up will continue to help. As the rich man planned out his future in the parable in Luke, God said to him, "Fool! This night your soul is required of you. So the things you provided, whose will they be?" (Luke 12:20) We need to serve, and we must do so today. Give the million away, do not put trust in the economy, and give up control of the future. The goal is to uproot our fear of need, not feeding other people out of our wealth.

Political systems of every leaning divert trickles of prosperity to the poor, but with a keen eye on themselves behind the dam. "They are prosperous," decries the left, "and some are not!" "We are prosperous," protests the right, "and we don't want less!" Both sides want their own pool to be safe; neither wants to tear down the dam. Left-leaning politicians create social programs but are careful not to upset wealthy friends. They love to take capitalism to the poor of the world, to teach them how to build their own dams.

Right-leaning groups claim they believe in the free flow of capital yet advocate more and bigger dams. Limiting immigration and reduction of welfare distribution are examples. In Europe, right-wing groups rally against immigration. "*Das Boot ist voll,*" "The boat is full," declares the German conservative Republican party, proclaiming that distribution of prosperity would lower the level of Germans' prosperity overall. In the United States, the Right argues against healthcare and welfare to the poor because they disincentivize them from working and working would add to the overall prosperity of the country rather than take from it.

People, moreover, hide incorrect actions behind the veil of institutions. Because they turn power over to the elite, they additionally abdicate to them the responsibility to act correctly. We imagine God and the government take care of the poor; we may help personally only as is convenient for us. We do not personally offer hospitality and alms to another human being, but rather we use the government's leaders to take care of the poor through housing and welfare. Rather than protect the poor, we expect a military to fight on their behalf, even though, as I showed above, the military recruits killers from among our own poor and "collaterally" kills the disempowered of other nations in the process. In our houses of worship, we pray to God to take care of the poor and put money in a box, so the church can take care of the poor for us. Hence, our "generosity" through paying taxes or tithes masquerades as fealty to God's Torah.

Humans righteously declare that duty binds us to do what we can to end suffering; nevertheless, our actions show that we do not trust that we could be sustained by the same means that we offer to the poor. As Jesus said of the Pharisees, "For they bind heavy burdens and grievous to be borne and lay them on people's shoulders; but they do not want to move them with one of their fingers. But all their works they do to be seen by people" (Matt 23:4-5). "Virtuous" individuals convince themselves that they can remain self-sufficient. Even worse, they become self-righteous, that they are helping the problem in a generous spirit. A geneticist will succeed in feeding more people but will continue to fill his house with food and possessions rather than move to India. The prayers of a religious person will be answered, and more will eat, yet she will remain confident that she can take care of herself as she walks through the grocery store instead of the food pantry. Politicians do not go on welfare. We all prefer the security of the salary and wealth that comes from our paycheck, rather than the abstractions we have invented for others. We count on our pool of prosperity, not on the natural flow we leave for others. With successful government, religion, and science, we smugly dam up prosperity for ourselves and deprive the foreigner and the unbeliever; we establish our self-righteousness as we establish the poor.

Introduction

In the midst of this lip-service about ending the suffering of others, we Americans work hard to keep the poor out of sight, away from us. We construct communities that the poor cannot access. We outlaw sleeping outdoors in the city, and suburban public spaces close at 10 p.m., rendering homelessness illegal. (Sleeping in jail is preferable, evidently.) We even invent public benches and ledges with arms and ridges on which it is impossible to sleep. We reject public transportation that could make it easy for them to come to our neighborhoods. We imprison panhandlers. We create neighborhoods—sometimes enclosing them with walls, fences, and guarded gates like a "fortified city"— that cost hundreds of thousands of dollars to live in. Poverty never confronts us. In contrast, poor people in Morocco walk through the narrow lanes of every neighborhood, literally calling for help and knocking on doors. In Ukraine, beggars create a gauntlet around the doors of churches on Sunday morning. Rather than remove the dams to serve the poor in front of us, we remove the poor from us and keep the dams.

Poverty is not the problem. We are the problem, surrounded by our pantheon of gods made by our own hands. Nature provides enough, but we usurp its power and prevent it from providing for all. We are not gods: we cannot help "poverty" any more than we can heal a dried-up river by adding water. Our fear of want creates the poor by taking more than our fair share.

The correct alternative—that no one takes—is the easiest, simplest approach to solving both questions: undam *our* abundance and let it flow naturally to those in need. The New Testament offers an example of how a self-righteous, materialistic yet religious person ought to act. When a man claimed that he observed all the commandments of Torah from his youth, Jesus commanded, "Everything you have, sell it and give it to the poor"

(Mark 10:21).[9] Jesus did not accept the religious observances the man claimed. They were the created gods of his own hands, the manipulation of God, not trust in him. Jesus demanded that the man trust completely in the abundance that God provides.

Once there was a waiter at a restaurant in the Middle East. A poor man approached him for food, and he sent him away. The owner overheard the conversation and quickly intervened. "At the end of the day we're going to throw away all this food, and you're denying him a piece of baklava?" he said as he handed the poor man a pastry. After the man left, the owner turned to the waiter and pointed to a sign written in Arabic hung on the restaurant wall: "*Al-mulku lillah*" "God is the owner."

Yhwh's proposition

Yhwh offers a proposition that undermines the entire human proposition, beginning with his supposition that he alone creates and controls the flow of prosperity. It was Yhwh who created the original bounty, Eden, and its four rivers, and placed the human being in its midst. Scripturally, humanity began with all the food it needed from the trees, all the water it needed from the rivers, and all the help it needed from the animals.

Humanity fell when this was not enough. Even though it was plenty for humans, they were tempted to desire more. The serpent tempted Eve with the idea that Yhwh was holding back, and if she ate of the tree of the knowledge of good and evil, then she would be like a god. All she lacked was divine knowledge. Not only were

---

[9] I purposely cited the version of this statement from Mark, rather than from Luke 18:22. The former introduces Jesus' interlocutor as "a man," while he is a "ruler" in Luke. We can all see ourselves in the Markan "man," whereas we might be tempted to imagine that a "ruler" has more of a duty to give up his wealth than we do. The judgment on our incorrect thinking comes down harder on the reader in Mark than in Luke.

humans dissatisfied with the food they were given—they wanted more fruit that was "good for food" and "pleasant to the eyes"—they were not satisfied with the knowledge they were given. It was not enough to know that they had enough; they needed to know everything, good and evil. We should note that everything up to that point had been pronounced "good"; "evil" had not yet been uttered.

A deity controls good and evil natural forces. In Hebrew טוב ורע, *ṭôv ve-ra'*, "good and evil," are not limited to moral categories, but also apply to the vicissitudes of natural forces. "Good" can be a bounty, for example, and "evil" can be calamitous events, such as poisonous food (2 Kgs 4:41) or general detriment (Jer 7:6). Human beings long to understand what good or evil might be coming to them, hence they invented divination. The quest to know, therefore, led them to reject their obvious prosperity to know what was coming next—good and evil. This ability to know would move them out of their inherently ignorant, human state.

The correct state would have been grateful acceptance of the bounty given without seeking to know what might come that could disrupt it. We should enjoy what we can without worry. As a result, we do not need a dam to ensure future prosperity against the good and evil that we humans know will come. Hoarding manifests knowledge that today is good, but tomorrow may be evil. Moreover, one does not need divination. One only needs to know the will of God concerning good and evil if one is anxious about continued prosperity. Outside of the Eden narrative, one only suffers once one rejects the proposal that one has—and knows—enough. Without the notion of scarcity, one does not need the dam for prosperity. One also does not need to worry about another person building a dam upstream.

In this mindset, manipulation of the source of prosperity becomes nonsensical. One fundamentally accepts what one receives. The one deity who created the heavens and the earth provides prosperity to all, if they are willing to accept it. He wanted humans to live in a perpetually prosperous garden with all the help they needed, before human beings grabbed the knowledge of good and evil. Furthermore, one cannot manipulate the one who alone controls good and evil. He has all he needs. No rites or sacrifices or rituals or prayers existed in Eden. In fact, the first inter-human conflict had sacrifice at its root, when Cain was jealous of the favor Abel received from Yhwh. Sacrifice and jealousy began at the same time.

In Yhwh's proposition, his favor and bounty are infinite. He can show favor on whomever he wishes and can provide bounty for anyone. The limitations come from us, just as they did with Adam, Eve, and Cain. The human paradigm turns upside down when one changes the supposition of fear to one of gratitude. "By God's grace I have enough; I have what I need." Without a dam or need for a dam, one walks up to the stream of prosperity and simply drinks.

Once we accept this proposition, human habits and institutions begin to crumble. We help the needy neighbor directly, since we assume we will never lack. Government is no longer needed. Distribution of wealth and prosperity happen naturally. The stream of prosperity flows on its own. Handing food along to the needy is simply the work of the stream of prosperity. Moreover, people would no longer need the defense that government provides. Military protection and violence would be superfluous. Humans would have no need to lash out in jealousy or desperation. We would not need to keep out foreigners, so maintaining the insider/outsider paradigm would no longer function.

Religion would likewise not function in a mindset of prosperity. As said above, divination would no longer serve any purpose. Rituals to manipulate the deity would not help if humans already have what they need. People would not feel the need to adhere to certain behaviors to prove their status to the deity, because the insider and the outsider would benefit equally from the bounty flowing to all. The feeling of being satisfied would likewise eliminate jealousy, removing another motivation for the insider/outsider paradigm.

The prosperity would, in the same way, remove the purpose of commercial science as we know it. The desire to create more food or resources would not exist. Perhaps humans would still be curious about how the cosmos functions, but there would be no existential problem to unlock.

If religion still performed a function, the purpose would be expressing gratitude. As religion began with anthropomorphizing a supposed limited source of prosperity, endless prosperity would come from a boundless, gracious deity. Either people would find no more need to imagine a divine source of prosperity, so ending religion, or they would thank the source for its infinite generosity. In the eschatological vision of Ezekiel, one would still sacrifice and celebrate the Passover (Ezek 45). Sacrifice would be practical—that is, feeding the central city—and spiritual—that is, offering up those things of high value, like bulls, rams, and he-goats.

Yhwh proposes trust in his prosperity. The amount of bounty stays the same, but humans must decide how to see it: with the assumption of prosperity or the assumption of insufficiency. The human heart since Adam inclines to the latter. Hence, Yhwh offers his Torah as the teaching that can lead us against our nature to accept his counter-human proposition and all the anti-religion and anti-government implications that accompany it. He does not offer increased bounty, but the ability to see that it already suffices.

The center of religion in this paradigm must be hearing Yhwh's teaching, listening to the reading of the book. Prayer puts the words into our mouths that our ego might deflate and that we act in accordance with the will of Yhwh that he communicated through Torah. Fasting only functions correctly when it is coupled with Yhwh's Torah. Almsgiving must embody the gratitude of the provision he offered freely; we thank him for his provision, but rather than eat it, we feed it to another. As we increase in Torah, we decrease as individuals.

Acting correctly defines one's righteousness or sin. "Righteousness" means accepting Yhwh's bounty, and "sin" consists of rebelling against the provider. The graciousness of Yhwh comes from the fact that prosperity is offered despite human righteousness and rebellion; the rebel can still enjoy prosperity, even if it is withheld for a time to move the rebel's mind back to the proposition of prosperity. Humans naturally fear insufficiency, even as Yhwh provides. They do not prosper because they deserve it, though. Yhwh offers prosperity out of his kindness, חסד, *xesed*, and thus enables—and expects—humans to respond with חסד, *xesed*, toward their neighbor. When a human sees another who might be wanting, he has the duty to act logically as one enjoying prosperity: he must give without hesitation. The human is obliged to keep prosperity flowing, and any prevention of flow constitutes rebellion and sin.

Present reality in light of Yhwh's corrective

Present reality confronts us with a problem: how can we reconcile Yhwh's infinite prosperity with the war, famine, and disease we see around us? The reality in human eyes is that prosperity is clearly limited, based on overwhelming evidence. Torah claims, however, that Yhwh controls all the forces of nature that could potentially limit prosperity. Any perceived lack thereof must be viewed as arising from Yhwh's will. What will a person do when faced with a threat? Will he search for the source of the threat, whether natural or human? Or will he recognize what Torah teaches, that the only source of any threat is Yhwh, trying again to remind his people of the importance of his instruction? Any threat is potentially pedagogical—will people learn?

In the face of calamity, people act incorrectly, as they inevitably become afraid and then make provisions for themselves. When the origin is natural, humans will go to a god—any god, whether Baal or genetic engineering—to ensure future prosperity. When the origin is human, such as war, humans will supplicate the enemy, fight him, or ally themselves with other people to fight against the common enemy. Yhwh does not accept the "natural" human reaction. When calamity comes, the prophetic voice insists, it comes from Yhwh.

The world in its natural state is empty; God fills it. From the initial creation of Gen 1, the world was chaotic waters until God (*Elohim*) filled it with land, plants, and animals. In an agricultural sense, uncultivated land is empty, covered with dust and brush—void of anything that gives life. Yhwh fills the land with water, crops for people, and hay for their herds. Yhwh's bounty turns the dry land into beautiful life.

Yhwh reminds all the people that he brought them into the land. He found them in a wretched, lonely state, and made them his children. They endured no ceremony, but a mere generous pronouncement brought them under the aegis of the one who created the heavens and the earth, who provides all, who controls the forces of destruction—in short, the one holding all power. The danger of foreign powers is they will exploit and use you, but Yhwh is different. While earthly powers need help building pyramids and cultivating fields, Yhwh needs nothing. Because he is completely self-sufficient—indeed, he supplies everything to everyone—he has no reason to exploit the people.

People display their ignorance of this fact when they go to other sources for help, so Yhwh needs to educate them time and again. He set the paradigm during the Exodus. When there was no food or water, he provided them. Yet the people complained about the food (Num 11). Moreover, they said the food was better in Egypt, implying that Pharaoh provided for them better than Yhwh, or at least better than Moses. In response to this complaint, Yhwh provided them quail for food, but at the same time, sent a plague against them. He thus demonstrated that he controls both prosperity and the lack thereof.

Yet Yhwh is exacting and demanding with his Torah. He commands that his people care for the widow, the orphan, and the stranger. He could take care of these people without assistance—and he does so continuously, without any gift from humans to gain his favor. It is not for himself that Yhwh requires this of people. Rather, the people benefit themselves. They build a society based on the abundance and mercy of Yhwh, which they pass on to the weak. In a society based on Torah, no one would be without because people become channels—rather than dams—of Yhwh's generosity. Since no such society exists, Yhwh continues to teach Torah through whatever means he sees fit.

When Yhwh appears to punish the people for not following Torah, he is, in fact, reminding them of his generosity. The people become greedy, manipulative, and exploitative as soon as they fear they may lack something, whether in the present or future. So they withhold, extract, and cheat the weak to strengthen themselves. Yhwh needs to remind them that they will always have enough because he controls it all. Anybody has anything because Yhwh gave it through generosity. Temporarily withholding his bounty from the people reminds them of the source of their abundance—and the inability to manipulate his favor.

Therefore, the human being must learn from deprivation. Yhwh gains nothing from providing or withholding. When a human finds that he has what he needs, he should thank Yhwh for his generosity and pass it to the poor. When he lacks, he should thank Yhwh for his generosity, continue to share what he has, and wait patiently for Yhwh to share again. Once the one who possessed what he needed learns what it means to lack, he gains the opportunity to become more sympathetic and hence more generous.

The role of the powerful: The king and the priest

In our response to his generosity, Yhwh only asks for one thing: חסד, *xesed,* "kindness." When Yhwh acted according to his חסד, *xesed,* and brought the Hebrews out of Egypt, they became his people, not free unto themselves. He took his people into slavery, but in a way entirely different from Pharaoh. They were bound to follow his will, his Torah, rather than Pharaoh's. He demanded that the priests and princes, the holders of power among the people, display חסד, *xesed,* and take care of the weak and poor.

The people themselves also had to show חסד, *xesed,* to the powerless, typified by the widow, the orphan, and the foreigner—all those who lack a human provider.

The powerful in society differentiate themselves as possessing the most to give, but the priests have a unique role. They mistakenly believe that they function primarily as cultic leaders. In fact, they serve as ministers of Torah. The priests are responsible for the people to know Yhwh's instruction. Even the king is subservient to Torah, and the priests are responsible for supplying the copy of the Torah before the king and for reading it to him (Deut 17:18-19). Once he has the knowledge of god, the king works simply as the chief slave of Yhwh's teaching, carrying out חסד, *xesed,* in every action.

Torah is more than rules, however: it is the story of Yhwh's dominion over creation and humans' continual betrayal. People betrayed—and continue to betray—him through rejecting his commandment, becoming jealous, relying on themselves, laughing at him, weeping in protest toward him, struggling against him, and searching for other providers whom they could see and control. All the while, Yhwh protected and provided for his people, occasionally chastising them. These two themes of Torah, betrayal and loyalty, must be drilled into the minds of the people, so the priest must never stop teaching.

The people, including the king and princes, witness to the teaching by their actions. They show whether the Torah is internalized—"in their heart," in biblical idiom—by acting accordingly. Do they follow the teaching of generosity and gratitude (חסד, *xesed*), or do they follow the teaching of coercion and fear? Do they offer their best to the powerful gods and kings through sacrifice and tribute, or to the weak through alms and hospitality? The people must respond to the teaching, but the priest initiates the action through teaching Torah. Since the people inevitably reject Torah through their actions, Yhwh must continue to teach them.

Book of Hosea and the Book of the Twelve

The human being at times finds himself in danger of lacking, caused by drought or foreign invasion. In the Book of Hosea, Israel finds itself at the brink of invasion and possible destruction by Assyria, as well as at risk of losing crops. In this reality, how can one accept the proposition of prosperity? Hosea seeks to answer this question. (Later, the Book of the Twelve takes on this problem further.) Israel's lack of security comes because they refuse the proposition of prosperity, which serves as a reminder of the prosperity enjoyed, but already forgotten. The prophet seeks to bring the people back to חסד, *xesed*.

In this work, I am assuming the Book of the Twelve is a single narrative in its canonical form.[10] All manuscript evidence we possess of the so-called Minor Prophets connects them with each other; we do not possess a self-contained scroll of a single Minor Prophet. Even at the risk of arguing *ex silencio*, we must entertain the possibility that the ancients viewed the Book of the Twelve as a whole. As a result, I will look at the Book of the Twelve as a single narrative made up of complete, individual mini-narratives. The scroll provides the correct frame for interpreting each one. Hence, Hosea contains a complete narrative, which also defines the dominant themes for the rest of the scroll.

The thesis of Hosea, and so the Book of the Twelve, is that humans' problems begin by rejecting Yhwh's Torah. Rather than

---

[10] I follow the Masoretic order of the Minor Prophets.

live under a deity who is never in need, they would enslave themselves to cruelly exacting gods and kings of their own making. Rather than construct a society of the powerful serving the weak, they would amass wealth and look over their shoulders, afraid of those who were more powerful. Rather than being provided for, they would provide for themselves. Rather than a light yoke of justice and mercy, they would prostitute themselves out to whoever might offer them any kind of favor. Acceptance of Torah grants them the life they want yet instinctively reject. The Book of Hosea confronts this lack of national logic.

The people were afraid of suffering. They feared agricultural privation caused by drought, flood, and invasion by pest. They equally feared military destruction, as they saw the rise of Assyria to the north and east.

They responded to these fears in the quintessential human way: they built institutions. They instituted a *quid pro quo* approach to religion in order to influence their gods. Hosea warned that Yhwh is the only god, who needs nothing from the people. Furthermore, they initiated diplomatic talks and offered gifts to pacify their bellicose neighbors. This might work in the short run, but even that is not guaranteed; as demonstrated in Joseph's time, those in power eventually forget that offering and enslave the weak.[11] The people must adhere to Torah and carry out mercy to the weak; otherwise, they had to trust Yhwh, the all-powerful, to take care of the rest.

With this important call to action—reject fear and the self-sufficiency that will supposedly relieve it—Hosea introduced the Book of the Twelve. The greater scroll narrates the struggle of

---

[11] See Exod 1:8-11.

Yhwh as he worked to establish his Torah in the earth. He gave it to the people, who chose self-sufficiency, war, and idolatry, and he caused them to lose in battle. Then the nations became particularly cruel because victory puffed up their ego, based on the illusion of self-sufficiency. They did not understand that they were the tool of Yhwh. Once Yhwh would teach the nations that Yhwh alone rules the entire world, he worked to crush their ego by withholding prosperity. Israel thus gained prestige in their own eyes, seeing their enemy crushed. When Israel's ego inflated, Yhwh crushed them again. Thus, Israel's and the nations' egos cycled on a continuous see-saw ride.

In the context of this pessimistic anthropology, the Book of the Twelve offers a solution: direct divine intervention. Eventually, Yhwh will usher in a new era, the eschaton, as he takes direct action to change the cycle of events. He will have to affect change directly in the human heart if he would hope for change. Yhwh will free humanity from its compulsive, self-imposed slavery to destructive forces by imposing his Torah in the last days.

Assumptions & Problems of Translation

The English text represents my own translation of the Hebrew, based on the traditional Masoretic text of *Leningradensis*. I have noted any departure from that manuscript. I am also following the Masoretic chapter and verse numbers. These do not always match the English numbering, especially in the early chapters, which I will mention in context.

Translating into English proves difficult because Hebrew words and phrases occasionally contain multiple meanings simultaneously. Proper names, because no capital letters exist in Hebrew, can be read as common nouns or phrases. For example, the word "baal" can either mean "husband" or it can be the proper name of a Canaanite deity.[12] The place-name "Jezreel" also carries its literal meaning, "God sows."[13] Hebrew writing can allow for multiple interpretations, because written vowels are more fluid than consonants. Not until the Middle Ages did the vowels come to be written consistently in biblical texts. When one changes the vowel on the word for "neighbor," for example, one arrives at "evil."[14] Hebrew syntax can produce multiple meanings, since, for example, "the living god" and "the god of life" are expressed the same way.[15] I believe that the Hebrew, like any language, can bear multiple meanings in a single unit, so I do not seek to eliminate any from consideration; often the multiple meanings underscore the author's point even more potently. In all of these cases, therefore, I had to choose a single meaning for the English translation, but I discuss in the comments the various ways that the word or phrase can be understood.

Other words refer to people, places, and events from elsewhere in the Hebrew Bible; these terms bear an intertextual meaning. While one can dispute whether the author intended to allude to these other passages, I draw out the intertextual meanings that arise for later readers. For example, ch. 6 mentions "Shechem." While this may have been a geographical location in the time of the author, it is the name of a man and of a place involved with significant events in the Bible, in Gen 35 and Judg 9. Thus, I will discuss how those events connect with the topic of ch. 6. By invoking a name or a place from elsewhere in the Bible, an intertextual reference can deepen or reinforce a point.

---

[12] See notes on 2:18.

[13] See notes on 1:4.

[14] See notes on 3:1.

[15] See notes on 2:1.

Introduction

Hebrew pronouns sometimes prove problematic for English translators. First, Hebrew possesses more pronouns than English. For example, Hebrew pronouns for the second person ("you") distinguish not only the number of addressees, like in many European languages such as French or Russian, but also gender. Thus, one pronoun is used when addressing a man, and another when addressing a woman, and this distinction allows a degree of specificity that does not exist in English.

Second, the author moved freely between second- and third-person pronouns ("you" vs. "they") to refer to Israel. In a single verse, the speaker may begin with what "you" have done and continue to talk about "their" actions. The text addresses two audiences: the internal and the external. The author wrote the story of a prophet speaking to a group of people, ancient Israelites whom we picture sitting in a city gate or standing in the marketplace. This is the imagined, internal audience. Adherents to the Bible believe that the text additionally addresses us and our contemporaries. This is the external audience. The *speaker* speaks to the internal audience inside the text, while the text presents their *interaction* to the external audience, outside the text. The switch in pronouns plays with the referents of "you" and "they," and so forces us to speak about the text on these two levels, internal and external, in order to understand first how the speaker in the text interacts with his audience, and second, how the text speaks to a modern audience.

In my translation, therefore, I preserved the peculiarities of pronoun-alternation, which enable the author to bring internal interactions to bear on an external audience. When it comes to gender, I will keep the reader informed of the pronoun to keep track of who is being addressed. Regarding switching grammatical person, the author simultaneously addresses a particular and universal problem. In other words, "he" and "they" refer to an other, the Israel of the text that may or may not be us. "You," however, addresses the audience within the text and invites its current hearer to listen as if he or she were an internal addressee. The actions of the external audience merge with the clear sins and consequences of the internal audience.

Regarding terms for the divine: the divine name, the Tetragrammaton, I have preserved as "Yhwh," rather than the traditional "LORD." This displays it as a proper name rather than a title. When I translate the Hebrew words אלהים, *'elohim,* and אל, *'el,* I used "god" or "God," depending on whether the context indicates that this is a common or proper noun, which are not distinguished in Hebrew writing, as I mentioned above. Much of the Book of Hosea explores which god, gods, or so-called gods the people turn to for help, and the Hebrew words for "god" carry more meanings than English. Sometimes it is a divine name, so in 4:1, for example, I use "God," because the context indicates that this is knowledge specific to the unique creator of the world. Other times, it can refer to any divine entity, so in cases such as "their god" (e.g., 4:6), I use the lower-case "god."

Each chapter of this commentary follows the same structure. I begin with my translation of the text, which includes notes on pronouns and basic translation choices. Then I introduce the major themes, followed by a verse-by-verse commentary. I conclude each chapter with implications of the text that connect to the following chapter.

Chapter 1

¹ *The word of Yhwh that was Hosea's, the son of Beeri, in the days of Uziah, Jotham, Ahaz, Hezekiah—kings of Judah—and in the days of Jeroboam, son of Joash, king of Israel.*

² *The beginning of Yhwh speaking by Hosea. And Yhwh said to Hosea, "Go, take for yourself a woman of whoring and children of whoring, for the land is whoring indeed from following Yhwh."*

³ *So he went and took Gomer, the daughter of Diblaim, and she conceived and bore for him a son.*

⁴ *And Yhwh said to him, "Call his name 'Jezreel,' for in a little while more I will visit the blood of Jezreel on the House of Jehu, and I will end the kingdom of the house of Israel.*

⁵ *"And it will come to pass on that day: I will break the bow of Israel in the Valley of Jezreel."*

⁶ *And she conceived again and bore a daughter, and he said to him, "Call her name 'Not Pitied,' for I will no longer be merciful to the house of Israel when I will surely take them away.*

⁷ *"But to the house of Judah I will be merciful and I will save them by Yhwh, their god. I will not save them by bow, by sword, or by war, by horses or by horsemen."*

⁸ *And she weaned Not Pitied and conceived and bore a son.*

⁹ *And he said, "Call his name 'Not My People,' because you are not my people and I will not be for you."*

The paternity test

Yhwh wanted to know if the people were truly his children, so he began with the confusion caused by an unfaithful wife. The characters played dual roles, as the prophet's relationship with his wife depicted the betrayal between Yhwh and the land. On the first level, the prophet represented the husband and the wife, Gomer, the whore. The "johns" of the whore were other men. Her children were Jezreel, Not Pitied, and Not My People, but we cannot know if Hosea or the johns were the father(s) of the children. On the next level, the mother was the land and the children were the people—the internal audience. The prophet was Yhwh and other men were other gods, so the question of paternity would be answered by determining which deity the people resemble.[1]

To determine paternity before the advent of DNA tests one examined the resemblance between father and child in looks and in habits. In the Book of Hosea Yhwh was thus putting the land to the test: Which of the mother's men did the children resemble?

The speaker described the state of the people by narrating their shameful lineage. They were the children of a whore, for whom the husband of the whore had no affection—for good reason. She was not a "reformed" whore, as the children were "children of whoring," that is, the children who resulted from unfaithfulness; their paternity was unknown. The husband, justifiably, did not immediately claim them as his. Metaphorically, the people were created out of an unfaithful land, and did not belong to Yhwh—unless he determined otherwise.

---

[1] Deuteronomy 31:16-21 described the land that the people would enter as full of other gods, after whom the people would turn. Hosea imagined these gods as lovers.

Chapter 1

A fertility myth reimagined

This first chapter turns an ancient fertility myth into a story of loyalty. Agriculture and human reproduction were seen as analogies of each other in the ancient world. For example, the English word for male reproductive cells, "sperm," derived from the Ancient Greek word, *sperma*, meaning both "seed" and "sperm." In a pre-biblical fertility myth, the god of agriculture copulates with the goddess of the earth and their union produces agricultural abundance.[2]

Ideally, Yhwh would have married the land, and she would have remained true to him, producing sons and daughters for him—but their births did not take place in this way. Children came from his wife, but he could not know whether they came from his seed. Yhwh would recognize if they came from his seed only if he could see their resemblance to himself.

The children began with two strikes against them. First, their mother was a whore. She was unfaithful and unable to trust completely in her husband. Second, the father of the children very well may not have been the prophet/Yhwh, but some other man/deity. The children thus shared their traits with this whore and their unidentified father. They would need to prove that Yhwh, from among all the candidates, was their father by acting according to his will.

---

[2] In the Sumerian fertility myth, the goddess Inanna and the god Dumuzi copulate as a metaphor for earthly fecundity. Inanna says in *The Courtship of Inanna and Dumuzi*, "As for me, Inanna / Who will plow my vulva? / Who will plow my high field? / Who will plow my wet ground?" Shortly after, the god is described, "At the king's lap stood the rising cedar / Plants grew high by their side / Grains grew high by their side / Gardens flourished luxuriantly" (Diane Wolkstein and Samuel Noah Kramer, *Inanna: Queen of Heaven and Earth: Her Stories and Hymns from Sumer* [New York: Harper & Row, 1983], 61).

The prophet knew he was marrying a whore, and presumed no pretense that she would be faithful. By analogy, Yhwh expected no faithfulness from the land. The children, as the offspring of such a mother, would not show faithfulness if Yhwh was not their father. Yhwh ostracized *her* children, symbolized by their names. This is a cold, unsentimental moment in ch. 1, as the husband openly rejected the children of his wife, after she openly rejected him. The children would have to prove their paternity. This family not only displayed dysfunction; they were founded on it.

While the ancient myths welcomed any fruit to come from the fertile land, Yhwh sought only one type of fruit: loyal children. In this chapter, the prophet's message was for the children, not the land. The land functioned as a literary device to present the nature of the internal audience, the people. The people may be "chosen," but this chapter assured them that it was not because of their glory. Their status came simply from the fact that they were born of Yhwh's wife.

A difficult message in a modern context

This scenario strikes the modern ear with an unpleasant sound of machismo and condescension. This husband "takes care" of a woman while shaming her and putting her in her place, reminding her of how great he is and how awful she is. To modern hearing, she did not "deserve" to be told this. The man did not possess the "right" to talk to anyone like that. We assume that he was oppressing her to inflate his own ego, and that he could not possibly benefit the woman.

By focusing on Yhwh's/the husband's actions, modern readers brush off the harsh critique against themselves. The prophet presented Yhwh's original, gracious actions towards the land and people, and contrasted their ungrateful actions. Whether Yhwh's judgment was acceptable to the audience is a secondary question that obscures the lesson in the text. If the land and people were reasonable, they would have remained faithful to their husband. The words of Hosea function to teach the people and judge their actions, not to place Yhwh on trial. Hearers of the text may well feel resentful towards Yhwh because they fixate on the messenger rather than on the message of their own unfaithfulness.

The resentful audience of the text does not hear her disloyalty, and so overlooks Yhwh's provision and protection. If he originally came to her entirely to help her, with nothing to gain for himself, then we have to hear this approach with different ears. If Yhwh was not coming to this situation to fill his own ego, we must assume a different motivation. His wife was already under suspicion of adultery; the children were the test. If the children, that is, the people, were in need, they would turn to the one they believed would provide for them. The one to whom they turned their loyalty, their trust, was their father. If Yhwh, in fact, took care of them, and the other would-be fathers did not, he offered them provision and protection *in spite of* their mother's disloyalty if they simply trusted that he alone would provide for and protect them in a way that no other god could.

The people could not understand Yhwh's gracious provision unless he deprived them first; we do not appreciate what we have till it is gone. They enjoyed his bounty for generations, yet they misunderstood where it came from. Rather than count on the god who provided everything for them, they tried to control their own source of life, and their need to control tyrannized them. By first removing the bounty, Yhwh began the process of freeing them.

Commentary

V. 1 While one usually reads this verse as simply a title listing people's names, it already invites a metaphorical reading. We can translate it as a series of common nouns and not as names. One can legitimately translate this verse, "The word of Yhwh that was for salvation, O offspring of my well!" since the name "Hosea" literally means "salvation." The book (both Hosea and the Book of the Twelve) is a word that brings salvation because it lays open for the people (inside the text) and for the reader (outside the text) the criteria of judgment and prosperity. The land brought forth life, the people, because Yhwh provided life in the form of water for the land to prosper. Furthermore, Yhwh's teaching offered a way for the people—and the reader—to flourish. Thus the people were the offspring of Yhwh's well. The people had an opportunity for salvation by learning from this word how their actions betrayed their loyalty.

V. 2 Yhwh began immediately with reference to whoring. Unlike Isaiah, who began with rebellion (פשע, *pesha'*), but resembling Ezek 16 and 23, who spoke of disloyal and ungrateful wives, Hosea began with the more visceral "whore" or "woman of whoredom." As a result, Hosea contextualized the relationship between Yhwh and the land not as sovereign and vassal, but as husband and wife, a more intimate relationship, heightening the betrayal. This theme appears throughout the Book of Hosea and informs every act of rebellion henceforth in the Book of the Twelve.

Significantly, Yhwh singled out the land as the whore, and did not refer here to the people. The land whored by cleaving to Baal, the Canaanite storm and fertility god. In ancient Near Eastern mythology, he provided the rain for the land to prosper. By coming together, the land and the rain, the land is impregnated and produces fruit. The people, then, benefitted from the land's relationship with Baal.³

Baal represented not only a fertility god, but also a warrior god.⁴ Baal usurped Yhwh's position as husband and as military protector, which suggests the reason for Yhwh to destroy Israel's weaponry in v. 5. Baal, therefore, was not only the agent of prosperity, but also of strength—in the mind of the people, at least. Who would the people turn to for prosperity and strength, Yhwh or Baal? The answer to this question weighs heavily on who their father is.

V. 3 The point of the marriage was not the relationship itself, but bearing children. Since the woman was known to be a harlot, Hosea could not be sure who the children's father was. This image implies that the people—represented by the children—would have to prove their paternity through loyalty, the central theme throughout the book.

V. 4 The first child's name, "Jezreel," literally, "God sows," indicated the way that the unfaithfulness of the land would play out in the next generation. On one level, the name expressed the intent of Yhwh to sow his seed in the "womb" of the land, that is, to produce children. Another man may have thwarted his intention, however. Since at least one man seemed to have gotten

---

³ As Wolfgang Herrmann wrote, "His elevated position shows itself in his power over clouds, storm and lightning, and manifests itself in his thundering voice.... As the god of wind and weather Baal dispenses dew rain, and snow...and the attendant fertility of the soil.... Baal's rule guarantees the annual return of the vegetation; as the god disappears in the underworld and returns in the autumn, so the vegetation dies and resuscitates with him" ("Baal," in *Dictionary of Deities and Demons in the Bible*, ed. Karel van der Toorn, Bob Becking, and Pieter Willem van der Horst, 2nd ed. [Grand Rapids, MI: Wm. B. Eerdmans Publishing, 1999], 134).

⁴ Mark S. Smith, *The Early History of God: Yahweh and the Other Deities in Ancient Israel* (Wm. B. Eerdmans Publishing, 2002), 79.

to Yhwh's wife first, someone else's children might be coming to "fruition."

On another level, the name referred to a specific event in 2 Kings, where humans betrayed Yhwh by adding their own word to his, and so they perverted justice. The Prophet Elisha sent one of the sons of the prophets to anoint Jehu as the leader of Israel and the destroyer of the current leadership of the people. Elisha told him the precise words to say, "Thus says Yhwh, 'I have anointed you king over Israel,'" followed by strict orders to "open the door, flee, and do not tarry" (2 Kgs 9:3).

The anointing prophet, however, acted treacherously to avenge his own brethren. Himself a son of the prophets, he was likely connected to the sons of the prophets whom Jezebel had previously ordered to be killed (1 Kgs 18:13). The prophet anointed Jehu and said his line as ordered in 2 Kgs 9:6, but in the following four verses he added an invective and curse that neither Elisha nor Yhwh told him to say. Rather than leave immediately, he spoke against Ahab and Jezebel by adding his own words, "I will avenge the blood of my servants, the prophets, and the blood of all the servants of Yhwh from the hand of Jezebel" (2 Kgs 9:7). Only in 2 Kgs 9:10 did he finally close the door and flee as originally commanded.

Even if Yhwh intended to remove King Joram, son of Jezebel and the champion of Baal, and put Jehu in his place, he did not authorize the prophet to order Jehu to kill Joram. Even though Yhwh previously predicted violence at the hand of Jehu (1 Kgs 19:16-17), these additional words were not a part of what the anointing prophet was to pronounce. The prophet overstepped his bounds, and Jehu carried out this vengeance at Jezreel with seeming glee mixed with religious fervor against Jezebel, their common enemy, and against the entire house of Ahab (2 Kgs 9:30-10:11). The sons of the prophets colluded with the new king to co-opt Yhwh's judgment and to corrupt justice.

While 2 Kings did not highlight this problem, Hos 1 did. Vengeance against Jehu is discussed only in Hosea. The judgement of Jezreel fit with the themes of Hosea because it represented conspiracy between prophet and king to benefit mutually at the cost of Yhwh's justice. The prophet told the king that vengeance comes from Yhwh, which allowed Jehu to fulfill his own ambition with impunity, believing that God was on his side. This is the blood that had to be avenged, and the son of Gomer, Jezreel, embodied this perversion. The twin ambitions of prophet and king showed that they were not sons of Yhwh, the god of justice, but sons of some father of bloody ambition.

These actions of Jehu and the adultery of the land's "other men" embodied the actions that thwarted Yhwh's will to producer his own fruit from the land. He wanted his own children to come from the land, and he wanted his leadership in place. The Baals, the prophets, and the king all followed their own wills and sowed their own seed. Hosea began with this as the original state of affairs, where Yhwh had to work that much harder for his will to be done.

V. 5 Yhwh promised to destroy Israel's ability to fight in war, and so end any perceived might of the king. Yhwh would reverse Jehu's victory over his enemies at Jezreel and show that the people would not be able to count on king or military to defeat their enemies—an ominous judgment that Yhwh would give victory to the enemies of Israel.

In light of the "test" that Jezreel, this son of unknown paternity, had to pass, Yhwh began by examining to whom this child would turn when his ability to defend himself was removed. Would he seek protection from the very one who broke his military might? The answer to this question would reveal the people's loyalty and, hence, paternity.

V. 6 Next came a daughter who signified that the children of this unfaithful wife would not receive pity from Yhwh. Until now, Yhwh was willing to provide for them and overlook their lack of loyalty, but no more. The paternity test would look at whom the people, namely, the House of Israel, followed when they no longer had Yhwh's protection. Upon their defeat, Yhwh would carry them away.[5]

V. 7 In contrast to the previous verse, Yhwh would have mercy on the House of Judah. First, Yhwh said in v. 6 that the daughter would not be pitied, while Judah was pitied here. Second, Yhwh said he would take away his protection from Israel, but here he said he would save Judah.

Yet the verse reinforced that the people could not possess any military means for salvation. In v. 5, Yhwh broke the bow of Israel. Here in v. 7 Yhwh promised to save Judah, but by himself and not by military means. Hence the people would rise and fall despite

---

[5] This verb, which usually has a neutral or positive sense, is difficult to translate in the current context, where it must have a negative meaning. It literally means "lift" or "carry"; for example, the waters "lifted up" (using this verb) the ark in Gen 7:17. In some contexts it has a positive, metaphorical sense, especially when followed by "iniquity" or "sin." "Bearing" the iniquity of the people is parallel to "covering" or forgiving sin in Ps 85:3. In Ezek 29:19, though, the verb contains a negative meaning, as the King of Babylon will "carry away" their multitude. I am reading this latter sense in Hos 1:6, understanding the preposition -ל, *l-* as marking the direct object. (See John Calvin's Commentary on the Bible for this verse: John Calvin, *Hosea*, trans. John Owen, Vol. 1, Commentaries on the Twelve Minor Prophets, [Grand Rapids: Christian Classics Ethereal Library, 2005], Hosea 1:6, accessed June 25, 2018, http://www.ccel.org/ccel/calvin/calcom26.viii.viii.html.)

Chapter 1

their military power. Once he breaks their military, he destroys their self-sufficiency, and only then can he save them.

We see the importance of reading this book in the context of the greater Book of the Twelve, because salvation would take place in the later portions of the Twelve. This verse indicates that Yhwh will save them by himself alone, and that the salvation will be merciful. The Book of Hosea did not indicate how or when this will take place, but we see later, for example, in Zech 2:5, that Yhwh will be the protecting wall of fire around Jerusalem—Yhwh himself, not a wall made by human hands. This mercy, however, will only come after a long story, told over the course of the Twelve, cycling between this people reaching great heights and falling to profound lows in the face of their enemies. Much as the mercy of Exodus came after 430 years of slavery (Exod 12:40-41), Judah will not see Yhwh's mercy until after many generations. The announcement of salvation is only the hope of good news.

Vv. 8-9 Gomer gave birth to a third child, whose name symbolized the end of the relationship between Israel and their god. While "Not Pitied" indicated the end of Yhwh's provision for Israel, the tie between deity and people was severed at this point. The people would be on their own.

The pronoun switched here in v. 9, so Yhwh addressed the people directly for the first time. Previously, he addressed only the prophet and referred to the people, the children, in the third person. Now Yhwh addressed the condemned directly.

Yhwh turned around the very language of Exodus to break this relationship. While in Exod 3:14, Yhwh said, אהיה אשר אהיה, *'ahiyê 'asher 'ahiyê*, "I am what I am," or "I will be what I will be," here Yhwh proclaimed, ואנכי לא אהיה לכם, *we'anokî lo' 'ahiyê lakem,* "and I will not be for you," or "and I am not the I AM for you." The disloyalty of the land, manifested in the children, reversed the relationship the Exodus established. Yhwh announced the functional reality when the actions of the people no longer reflected that they considered Yhwh to be their god.

The final son completed the narrative of the three children: God Sows, Not Pitied, and Not My People. When God sowed, the fruit came up as children who wanted to wrest control of God's words for themselves, as was seen at the field of Jezreel. Yhwh withdrew his pity, and the people would see that without him, they could no longer hold on to the illusion of control. As the people no longer acted as if Yhwh was their god, their god withdrew from them.

Judgment, not chosenness

Their maternity is clear: they were the sons of a whore; therefore, their paternity was unclear. The people desired prosperity and strength, but they showed in Jezreel that they wanted to use Yhwh's words and judgment to their own ends. Hos 1 focuses on the past unfaithfulness of the land, however, and the potential disloyalty of the people; they started out with a strike against them. As a result, Yhwh would test them by withdrawing from them, removing first his mercy and second his divine oversight. This chapter sets out the beginning of the history of the children of Israel. The narrative begins with the parents of the people, and moves through the judgment.

The chapter removes from the outset any notion of "chosenness" from the people, and lays out the conditions for the paternity test. They were bastard children and disowned by the very deity who they believed chose them. Even Judah, who seemed to receive a slight reprieve in v. 7, found itself in an awkward position. Yhwh would break the military might of Israel, but he would show mercy on and save Judah without military might. Any reliance on military might would negate this promise. They could not add words to Yhwh's promise, they could not look to any means of provision, and, most of all, they could not look to themselves for salvation.

Chapter 2

¹And the number of the sons of Israel will be like the sand of the sea that will not be counted or numbered, and it will come to pass in a place where it used to be said to them, "You are not my people," that it will be said to them, "Sons of the living god."[1]

²And the sons of Judah and the sons of Israel will be gathered together, and they will set one head for themselves, and they will go up from the land, for great is the day of Jezreel.

³Say to your brothers,[2] "My people," and to your sisters, "Pitied."[3]

⁴Contend with your mother, contend, for she is not my wife, and I am not her husband, so she will turn away her harlotries from before her, and her adulteries from between her breasts,[4]

⁵Lest I strip her naked and establish her like the day of her birth, and I make her like the wilderness, set her like a dry land, and kill her with thirst.

⁶And her sons I will not pity because they are the sons of harlotry.

⁷For their mother has harloted. Shamefully she conceived them, for she said, "I will go after my lovers, the givers of my

---

[1] This is 1:10 in English Bibles.
[2] All the second-person references in this verse are in the plural.
[3] This is 2:1 in English Bibles.
[4] All the second-person references in this verse are in the plural.

bread and my water, my wool and my flax, my oil and my drink."

⁸Therefore, I am hedging up your way with thorns. So I will wall up her wall, and her paths she will not find.[5]

⁹And she will pursue her lovers, but she will not overtake them, and she will seek them, but she will not find them. So she will say, "I will go and return to my first man, because it was better for me then than now."

¹⁰And she did not know that I gave her the grain and the new wine and the oil. Silver I multiplied for her, yet gold they made into Baal.

¹¹Therefore, I will turn and take my grain in its time, and my new wine in its season. And I will take away my wool and my flax to cover her nakedness.

¹²And now I will reveal her lewdness in the eyes of her lovers and no man will deliver her from my hand.

¹³And I will end all of her joy, her holiday, her new moon, her Sabbath, all her feasts.

¹⁴And I will destroy her vine, and her fig tree, which she said, "They are a present to me that my lovers gave me!" And I will make them a forest and the beast of the field will eat them.

¹⁵And I will visit upon her the days of the Baals to whom she burned incense. And she put on her earring and her jewel, and

---

[5] The second-person reference in this verse is in the feminine singular.

Chapter 2

she went after her lovers. But me she forgot. The oracle of Yhwh.

¹⁶Therefore, behold I am alluring her, and I will lead her to the wilderness, and I will speak to her heart.

¹⁷And I will give her vineyards to her from there, and the Valley of Achor for an opening of hope. And she will answer there like the days of her youth and like the days when she went up from the Land of Egypt.

¹⁸And it will come to pass on that day—the oracle of Yhwh—you will call me "my man," and you will not call me any more "my husband."⁶

¹⁹I will turn the names of the Baals from her mouth, and they will no longer be remembered by their name.

²⁰And I will establish for them a covenant on that day with the animal of the field, and with the bird of the air, and with the creeping thing of the ground; and bow and sword and war I will destroy from the land, and I will make them lie down in security.

²¹And I will betroth you to me forever, and I will betroth you to me in righteousness, and in justice, and in kindness, and in mercy;⁷

²²And I will betroth you to me in faithfulness, and you will know Yhwh.⁸

---

⁶ The second-person references in this verse are in the feminine singular. בעלי, *baʻali*, which I have translated "my husband," also means, "my Baal." See commentary, below.

⁷ The second-person references in this verse are feminine singular.

⁸ The second-person references in this verse are feminine singular.

²³And it will come to pass on that day that I will answer—oracle of Yhwh—I will answer the heavens, and they will answer the land,

²⁴And the land will answer the grain, the new wine, and the wool, and they will answer Jezreel.

²⁵And I will sow her to myself in the land, and I will show mercy to Not Pitied, and I will say to Not My People, "You are my people," and he will say, "My god."⁹

Grammatical note

As I mentioned above in the Introduction, Biblical Hebrew makes a distinction among second-person references, that is, it uses multiple words translated into English simply as "you." I have indicated in the footnotes the three distinct second-person forms of address used in this chapter: masculine singular, feminine singular, and plural. I would recommend that the reader unfamiliar with Biblical Hebrew follow these changes in address carefully, as they indicate different immediate addressees in this chapter.

When one reads only in English, the changes in address can lead to mixing the characters completely. As I follow the text verse-by-verse, I will show how the text grants the characters independent life.

Apostasy in mythological terms

Israel's actions will make their paternity unambiguous: they are sons of Yhwh or sons of Baal. They believed that each god offers them prosperity in his own way, so they bowed to each one to

---

⁹ The second-person reference in this verse is masculine singular.

receive the full complement of what they wanted. The people may choose to worship more than one god, but the prophet laid out a story that made this choice logically impossible. One father sired them; the role of "life-giver" cannot be shared.

The fate of the land and the people were inextricably intertwined, as Hosea depicted apostasy and its effects through mythologizing the deuteronomic blessings and curses. In Deuteronomy, we see how Yhwh protected the people as long as they did not follow other gods; otherwise, the land would not provide blessings but curses (11:22-28). Yhwh commanded the people to obey his commandments so that he might make them victorious over other nations and possessors of the land (vv. 22-25). In fact, we may want to consider the other possessors of the land as inheritors, since the land only belonged to Yhwh, and was meted out by his will. According to their actions, the people would experience a blessing if they obeyed or a curse if they disobeyed (vv. 26-28). The curse would come if they chose to go after other gods (v. 28).

In Hosea's narrative, the land and people are characters, mother and children. Verse 4 of the current chapter addressed the children, that they might "contend with" their mother, the wife of Yhwh. Hence the mother continued as the image of the land. We also saw in ch. 1 that her children were the people of Israel whose mother's unfaithfulness started them off in a state separated from Yhwh: Jezreel, Not Pitied, and Not My People.

The act of following after the Baals is depicted as children paying homage to their father, who was not the husband of their mother. The children caused their wayward mother—the land—to be stripped of her fineries, to be cursed. The test of the children to establish justice around the land's adultery required that everything be taken from them. The mother's adultery and the children's suspiciously Baal-looking behavior led them to experience the "curse," stripping the goodness of the land, like stripping this woman, their mother, naked. Hence the land was not simply "bare," but exposed and ashamed. By worshiping Baal, the land and people conspired together against Yhwh.

One must understand the mythological framework of this text to answer the question, "How does a land declare its faithfulness, in word or in deed?" The mythological context contemporary to the Bible offers a precedent to such an idea, in addition to what I mentioned in the last chapter. Fertility comes from the strength and presence of the reigning deity. In Ugaritic mythology, Baal, the god of fertility, fought against Mot, the god of death and deserts. When Baal vanquished the latter and presented himself on Mount Saphon, the land was fertile.

The real problem in Hosea was less the so-called choice of the land to follow Baal, but the worship of Baal by the people, because they make Yhwh non-functional. The story of Yhwh and the story of Baal are incompatible. In contrast to the story of Baal, Yhwh alone resided in the heavens reigning over the earth—both of which he created by himself. Yhwh was the god of life and of death. There cannot be two fertility gods. Moreover, Baal received his power from his father, El; Yhwh created everything himself. The mythology of Hosea forced the addressees into a logical problem: Baal and Yhwh cannot both give life, any more than a land can have two kings sitting on the same throne, or a child can have two biological fathers. The land was faithful to Yhwh when she turns only to her husband for provision and not to her boyfriend, Baal.

The text thus addressed the issue of hedging one's bets, rather than committing to one story or another. Humans always hedge their bets. Whether they both built grain stores and prayed to the storm god, or both created a retirement savings account and prayed to God on Sundays, they did not put all their chips on a single number. They trusted themselves to make a good decision rather than a single god to make the decision for them on a daily basis. The addressee of this book, ancient or modern, does not want to commit to a single deity and his story of supremacy. In this way "Baal" represents any mode of giving prosperity besides Yhwh alone. As the people lived in the land, they wanted to pray to whoever would get them what they wanted, and were not choosy about who got it for them or how. They simply wanted those things that offered a good, comfortable life. Instead, Yhwh demanded loyalty.

Apostasy and marriage

Marriage may not bring all good things immediately, but in order to bear fruit, loyalty to the partner must come first. A cheating husband or wife who seeks his or her own comfort—wherever he or she might find it—before loyalty will only bring misery upon him- or herself, and will receive only bad things as a result. In our modern society, people who are not getting their "needs met" in a marriage have a license to leave their marriage to meet those needs elsewhere. Loyalty to personal "needs" precedes loyalty to the spouse. The land followed the same path: she went where she got the good things. In life under Yhwh, just like in any marriage, difficult times arise on occasion, and loyalty must remain top priority.

If children demand their personal material well-being, and reject their father, the family cannot prosper until the father brings them into line. In Hosea the children and mother dishonored the mother's husband and children's provider. The children should have demanded loyalty of their mother towards her husband, and not encourage infidelity.

Commentary

V. 1 Only one deity, Yhwh, gives life; hence the people will be "sons of the god of life." This title contrasted him with Baal, the god of the Canaanites, whom the Israelites ignorantly believed gives life.

This title of Yhwh's can be translated multiple ways, which underscores how Yhwh held all prosperity, and thus life, in his hand. I translated it "the living god," because he did not depend on any source of life; he lived while all life depended on him. One can also translate it as "the god of life," which adds the connotation that life comes from him. Baal may have been the god of the storm, but Yhwh is the god of life itself. Finally, the word for "god" can be read as the proper name, "El," the head of the Canaanite pantheon and the father of Baal; thus, we can read it as "the living El" or "El of life." Yhwh thus asserted himself as the true head of the gods, the El who gives life—unlike the other El the people may have heard of. This epithet thus placed Yhwh at the top of any pantheon the people imagined, as the singular source of prosperity and life.[10]

When the relationship was ordered correctly, Yhwh was the only father and husband and life abounded. The sons of Israel would be like the "sand of the sea" in number. This image is used in

---

[10] This phrase also occurs in Josh 3:10, when Joshua exhorts the people to enter the land, knowing that the "god of life" will drive out the Canaanites residing in the land. This context foregrounds the military aspect of Yhwh.

Genesis[11] and Isaiah[12] as the ultimate success for Israel, and elsewhere it refers to overwhelming military forces.[13] If the people upheld their end of the promise, and Yhwh his end, then the people would number more than one can count; the people could succeed. Such life naturally depended on the good things of the land, food, clothing, and so on, which they could not receive if the land was cursed due to their apostasy.

V. 2 The reversal of the people's fortunes would continue. Remembering that the original day of Jezreel was a mockery of what Yhwh was supposed to have sown, the future day of Jezreel will be "great."[14] Previously, God was supposed to have sown, but the fruit of Baal came forth. The fruit of Yhwh will arise next time, as it was supposed to. Children who resemble him will be born. King Jehu unjustly usurped the leadership because of ambitious prophets who spoke falsely in the name of Yhwh. The reversal, then, is a unified leader for both Judah and Israel who seeks true justice for others. Justice would replace ambition.

V. 3 As the curse of Jezreel is transformed, so would the curse of the rest of the children. Thus, "Not My People" would be "My People," and "Not Pitied" would be "Pitied." Once the sowing of God would produce children who are loyal to him, the separation would be nullified.

---

[11] Gen 32:13; 41:49.

[12] Isa 10:22; 48:19.

[13] This phrase can refer to a frightening array of enemies: Canaanites in Josh 11:4; combined Canaanite forces in Judg 7:11; Philistines in 1 Sam 13:5. It refers to Israel in 2 Sam 17:11, as an army against Absalom. It is a peaceful image in 1 Kgs 4:20, when the people are eating peacefully under Solomon's rule. One time it does not refer to people, in 1 Kgs 5:9, where it depicts Solomon's wisdom from Yhwh.

[14] See notes on 1:4.

The question is one of loyalty versus disloyalty, which hinges on what type of action Jezreel takes. Will the people use Yhwh—or whatever god they choose—to their own ends to get what *they* want, or will they submit to Yhwh, whether or not they approve of his actions?

This is the paternity test for Yhwh. Does one use the gods to authorize one's own words to get what one wants, or does one stick to Yhwh and his word to do what he wants? While this opposition was exemplified by Jezreel, it was not exclusive. Baal represented any will besides that of Yhwh. Any usurpation of Yhwh's will displays one's Baalic paternity; sons of Yhwh by definition show fealty to Yhwh's will alone.

V. 4 The people's obedience to Torah, Yhwh's will, will bring the land back into the correct state. Once the children are truly Yhwh's, they will no longer laud the Baals, and so their mother will no longer dally with other gods. Previously, the children worshiped Baals and entreated the land through cultic actions to couple with Baal; now the faithful children entreated their mother to remain faithful to Yhwh. The consequences carry on into the next two verses.

V. 5 The land would bear the consequences of the people's disobedience, as this verse continues the thought of the previous verse. If the mother did not remain faithful to Yhwh at the entreaty of the children, then she would no longer be fruitful. She would be bereft of crops, fruit, and animals as Yhwh ceases to provide water. He would show that Baal was not providing water and fertility; he was. He can prove that he alone was providing water and fertility by depriving the land of both. She will be like a land that was not sown by Yhwh, the opposite of "Jezreel."

V. 6 If the land was not producing life, it was because she strayed from her husband, Yhwh. If the children acted like true children of Yhwh, they would be contending with their mother to go back to Yhwh. They seemed to be encouraging their mother to go with the Baals. If they were not encouraging the land's coupling with Baal, she would still be enjoying the good things of Yhwh. They would be children of harlotry—not Yhwh's—and so be cursed by him. As a result, the children will revert to "not pitied" and "not my people."

Thus, the children bore some responsibility of the state of the land, and the state of the land had dire consequences for them. The text implies that when the people offered sacrifices to Baal (even if they thought it was Yhwh), they liturgically tried to bring the land and Baal together. If they had followed Yhwh's Torah, they would have encouraged coupling between the land and Yhwh, providing what they needed.

V. 7 This verse shows the mentality of apostasy: one forgets who provides agricultural bounty. The source of the land's problem was that she believed that her lovers—not her husband—brought her good things: sustenance (bread and water), clothing material (wool and flax), and luxury items (oil and wine).[15]

The children had to contend with their mother so that she might stop this behavior and return to her husband. The mother fixed her mind on harlotry, and her actions lay at the basis of the charge of harlotry. Therefore, Yhwh was testing the children's paternity. The children had a responsibility to follow his will and to turn

---

[15] All of these items come directly from the ground, except wool, but the sheep from which it comes depend on the abundance of growth from the ground.

their mother back to her husband if they wanted to pass the paternity test and prosper in the land.

V. 8 Yhwh promised to deliberately make the lives of the people more difficult, to see to whom they would turn, whether they would work to turn their mother back to her husband. The judgment against the people/children was bound with that of the land/mother, so Yhwh would restrict the movement of both. The verse addresses the people/children, represented by a single, male addressee, and the land/mother in the third person. As a result, the mother and children would no longer be able to wander after her lovers, penning them in with thorns. On the one hand, Yhwh restricted freedom, but on the other, he removed temptations to wander.

The image of thorns served double duty as an image of a pen for livestock and of infertility and drought. To this day, traditional herding societies create barriers for herd animals out of thorns in areas that lack trees for wooden fences—often dry, drought-stricken areas. These thorns would therefore fence in the wife from wandering. Elsewhere in the Bible, the replacement of crops with thorns displays Yhwh's judgment. The land would bring forth plants that were useless and difficult to remove, rather than for food. Adam's labor was cursed to bring up thorns rather than fruit (Gen 3:18). In Isa 34:13, thorns would grow up in the palaces, weeds that begin to take over the human structures that Yhwh has emptied of people. This section of Hosea thus uses an image to double for fences and drought to explain the judgment against the land, which subsequently deprived the people.

V. 9 The pen would only work temporarily; it could slow the mother but could not stop her. The effort and payoff, though, may not be worth it, as she decided to turn back to her "first" man.

The word אִישִׁי, *'îšî*, can mean "my man" or "my husband." I translate this as "my man" because she did not differentiate among her lovers; they are simply numbers in a sequence. Things were working best when she was with her first man rather than when she was with her other men, so she decided to go back to him. Leaving her first god caused her problems; nevertheless, converting will not spring her from the prison her actions have generated, so coming back to him will not end her life of "thorns."

V. 10 Yhwh explained the deeper source of the problem, however: her ignorance. She knew that the situation was better with her first man, but she did not know that even when she was supposedly in the protection of the others, Yhwh was still the one providing for her. While she thought her other men provided for her less than Yhwh did, Yhwh stated that they provided nothing for her. Everything came from him, no matter whom she was with.

The people, the children, followed this misinformation. While she misunderstood where the bounty came from, her children offered it up to Baal. This is the reason for the change in pronoun mid-verse, from "her" to "they." The children furthered their mother's mistake. Instead of dedicating back to Yhwh the bounty that he was providing, they offered it up to their biological father, Baal.

The children encouraged the mother's unfaithfulness. They created and worshiped the golden Baals so that their mother would couple with her lover. The people's cultic apostasy displayed not only rebellion but furthered their mother's ignorance. They followed her in her misunderstanding of the source of good things. Their fate was tied intimately with the attitude of ignorance, and the resulting judgment of their mother.

V. 11 As introduced in v. 8, the judgment began against the land. Both verses start with the same "therefore," and this structure verbally connects the hedging from v. 8 and the current deprivation. Yhwh would take away what she sought from him when her lovers could not provide them: the grain and wine, the food and the drink. Then he will take away the clothing, leaving her naked and ashamed. Metaphorically, flax and wool cover the mother's body as clothing, but literally, they cover the land in the form of crops and flocks. Their god will remove the bounties from her, leaving her humiliated, in a metaphorical sense, and barren, in a literal sense. The curse, then, worked against the mother and the children.

V. 12 Once Yhwh would uncover her, her lovers would see her, and she would be ashamed. Rather than allure them, her nakedness would repulse them. The Hebrew can be read "no one" or "no man (will deliver her)." The latter makes more sense in the context. In v. 9, she thought that any man could provide for her, though one perhaps provided better than another. Only Yhwh had the power to provide—and to deprive.

V. 13 Judgment would end all joy for her. The text designates all the festivals as "her," the mother's, not "their," the mother's and the children's. One would expect the cultic part of the relationship to be expressed by her children, because the people celebrated on these days. The land could not celebrate on its own, so one would expect here "their holiday," "their new moon," etc.

The people, however, celebrated the bounty of the land on these days. The items used in the cult to praise the provider came from the land. The people did not possess a holiday; the land possessed it and the people derived their festivals from the land.

V. 14 Further expressing her ignorance, the woman believed that her produce—vine and fig tree—were offered to her from her lovers for her services. Yhwh expresses his control over the land through removing the good things. They are not from other men; they are from him. He will allow field and flock to be overgrown by forests and beasts of the field.

V. 15 The people's worship caused the problem. The people may have thought they were celebrating the bounty of the land in the festivals of v. 13, but they in fact expressed and celebrated the land's harlotry. Yhwh judges her reliance on the Baals, whom she sought to seduce with the good things Yhwh gave her. She used to dress up to pursue them shamelessly. She sinned in two ways: one, she did not remain faithful to the one who gave her good things; two, she used those very items to entice other gods, her supposed providers. He will visit her, not with good things, as before, but with a judgment, as described in vv. 4-14. The fancy displays that the people put on aimed at themselves and the Baals, not for Yhwh.

The same confusion of v. 13 appears here because one would expect that the children, not the wife, would burn incense to the Baals. The children created the idols in v. 10. Incense, however, is not limited to cultic settings, but is also used as a way to entice men to the bedroom. In Ezek 16:18 and 23:41, both depicting a similar story of Yhwh's unfaithful wife, incense was "set up" to allure her lovers. In the current verse, the incense was being used as a scent to delight the senses of the Baals.

V. 16 Yhwh will turn the tables. As this verse, like vv. 8 and 11, begins with another "therefore," the narrator presented a third result of the apostasy. Yhwh would allure her, as she allured other men, but with two twists. First, he will take her to the desert. She wanted to bring him to a place of her fineries, but he will bring her to a rough place without any civilization. Metaphorically, this man will lead the wife to a place without distractions, without lovers, so he can "level" with her. Literally, since a land cannot move, Yhwh will turn the land into a מדבר, *midbar*, "wilderness." The "visitation" of judgment would be used to scold her, but it was also the situation in which he would speak to her. Once the land had no provision whatsoever, she would depend on him and hear his word.

Second, he would reason with her. The ancients understood the heart to be the center of the intellect, not feeling. He is thus not "romancing" her when he speaks to her heart. The original problem arose because she did not understand, because she forgot Yhwh provided for her (v. 10).[16] Once she depends completely on him, she will be able to listen and maybe understand.

V. 17 Yhwh offered hope upon speaking to her in the מדבר, *midbar*, "wilderness," as he would begin to restore her bounty with vineyards and the Valley of Achor (Hebrew for "trouble"). When Yhwh brought the people out of Egypt into the wilderness, he controlled the land completely, and she prospered. The land provided a bounty to the people without the normal things one would expect, such as rain and fertile soil. He showed that he could make the land prosperous by his will alone. She submitted to his power and enjoyed her situation, until she finally started dallying with other gods who were promising prosperity to her. Yhwh promised that on this second trip to the desert she will

---

[16] In Zech 12, Yhwh poured out his spirit on the people so they would understand the error of their ways. Both examples from the Book of the Twelve depict Yhwh trying to help the people understand the reality of the situation. (See Richard Benton, "The Pain of Victory: The Identity of the Pierced One in Zechariah 12:10," *Journal for the Orthodox Center for the Advancement of Biblical Studies*, 7 [2014]: 1–12.)

respond more faithfully, as she did in her "youth," before she became entangled with lovers.

The metaphor, however, becomes confusing here when it describes her coming up from the Land of Egypt, as the metaphorical wife was not in Egypt, and the literal land could not move from one place to another. At this point, interpreting the people as the wife—and reading that back into v. 16—is tempting. Moreover, the Hebrew consonants can be read "like the day she came up from," as well as, "like the day of her coming up from."[17]

The land came up from Egypt when she became Yhwh's land, once he laid claim to her. In the previous verse, we understood that Yhwh was not leading her back to the מדבר, *midbar*, "wilderness," of Egypt, that it was a metaphorical trip. When the people came out of Egypt, the land became Yhwh's as he possessed her and caused her to flourish, so he could sustain his children through her. "Milk and honey" do not represent natural attributes of the land, but the bounty that Yhwh creates.[18]

V. 18 At that time she would change how she addresses Yhwh. She was calling him "my Baal," which is a play on the Hebrew word. "Baal" is a proper name of a Canaanite deity, as well as a common noun meaning "husband." The word would no longer cross her lips, even with the second meaning, lest any ambiguity arise. Instead, she would call him "my man." This is a strong contrast from v. 9, where she called him "my first man." He would be her exclusive man—as a husband should be.

---

[17] A straight perfective (*qatal*) reading of the verb underscores the problem.
[18] In the same way, Yhwh promised to make the Valley of Achor a place for grazing in Isa 65:10.

V. 19 After Yhwh talks some sense into the land, she will return to her young, pristine state, as before she went astray (v. 17). She would no longer even remember that there are other men, or other ways to seek prosperity. Only one would be in her mind. The names of Baals were the names of "husbands," which we see in the different manifestations of Baal in the Bible, such as Baal-peor (Num 25:3) and Baal-zebub (2 Kgs 1:2). These Baals, whether deities or husbands, caused the people to misplace their loyalty.

V. 20 The people would peacefully prosper in the land, once the land returned to her senses. We see the shift in pronoun, from "her" to "them," indicating that the author shifted focus from mother to children, from land to people. Yhwh would again provide for the people by establishing a covenant with all potential enemies, supplying bounty and protection to the land. He would return nature to a benign state, reversing v. 14. He would destroy all weapons from the land. Even though he destroyed Israel's bow in 1:5, now war and its instruments would be completely gone from among the people.

Vv. 21-22 The identifying feature of Yhwh, in his land and, one assumes, in his children, was justice, kindness, mercy, faithfulness, and knowledge of Yhwh. We can understand these qualities in two ways. First, when he betrothed her to himself, she was to be his exclusively, and so these five qualities would abound. Second, he offered these items to his bride in exchange for her hand in marriage. The Hebrew verb ארש, '*aras*, "betroth" can take the preposition -ב, *b-* to mean "for," indicating a dowry, such as when King David betrothed Michal "for" 100 Philistine foreskins. Thus, we see the exchange: Yhwh would offer these good things for the dowry, gifts for her to possess and use.

If these are the identifying features of the father, then we would expect to see these traits in the children, if he is truly their father. Again, we remember the ancient paternity test. We must assume that the children resemble their father, and so children of Yhwh would manifest justice, kindness, mercy, and faithfulness, and by this the wife will observe—"know"—Yhwh.

Vv. 23-24 The land will be sown correctly in the future, and the people will come out correctly. Yhwh's actions would start the chain of events that communicated the new state of affairs that would come after Yhwh speaks to the land to change her mind. The heavens, the abode of Baal and the rains, would know first, once Yhwh testified to them of his power over them. This dominance would answer the land, who was looking for a husband who would provide for her. In turn, her faithfulness to the master of the heavens would answer the produce of the land, who would prosper because of her loyalty. Finally, the question of "Who sowed the soil?" that was asked of Jezreel would be answered.[19] Faithfulness will have trickled down through all the relationships mentioned, resulting in Yhwh's prosperity as well as all the other gifts of Yhwh: justice, kindness, and mercy.

V. 25 The paternity will be confirmed, and the children of the land will be Yhwh's. Yhwh affirmed that he sowed the field, so "Jezreel" and the children must necessarily be his. Hence, he will bestow on them mercy and possession onto them. Furthermore, since they were loyal, they will return to him their loyalty, declaring him alone to be their god.

---

[19] See the discussion on 1:4, above.

Return to senses

The confrontation with "Jezreel" would determine the fate of the people. Was "Jezreel" true, that is, would the land show that "God sowed"? Or would "Jezreel" prove to be the point of rebellion, once the son of another was born of the land? The original sin in Jehu's time tilted the situation away from the people's favor.

Yhwh would devastate the land as both her judgment and her hope. The text arranged this in three sections with the key logical indicator, "therefore." After the description of her offense in v. 7, the text presented the result in three complementary ways. First, he would pen her in with thorns, so she could not pursue her lovers (v. 8). Second, he would take away all prosperity (v. 11). Third, he would seduce her again, providing for her in the מדבר, *midbar,* "wilderness," where she had nothing (v. 16). She and her children would see that they could do nothing to provide for her through other gods and their own means. When they have nothing, only Yhwh provides.

Prosperity began with Yhwh's word, but next came correct understanding. In the last of the phases in v. 16, Yhwh was speaking sense to her. When her mind would be changed, no thought or word of Baal would occur to her, just like before she had ever heard of the Baals. At that point, her children would live a good life.

In order to recognize children as belonging to Yhwh, they had to display his characteristic traits: justice, kindness, mercy, and faithfulness. Their conduct to this point had been questionable, and Yhwh had to determine whether they were his or not. His wife's conduct made the question necessary, but the process of determining the truth was difficult.

Chapter 2

Yhwh had to break down his wife before she could be built back up because her rebellion was rooted in ignorance. She mistakenly believed that every "man" could provide for her in his own way, but in reality, Yhwh alone provided everything. This basic change in thinking could transform her from a whore to a faithful wife, as she was in the beginning, when he first married her, and as the people were "born."

The people must live in obedience to the teaching and will of their father. This chapter confronted the land, the mother, to change her way of thinking, as well as to the children to convince her to turn back. The children were guilty of going after their mother's lovers, as well, and creating images out of gold. If all would be successful, the land would return to a pristine, fruitful state, displaying the woman's fineries, as well as providing handsomely for the children, who would clearly resemble their father, Yhwh, in their obedience. They would prove he is their father.

Chapter 3

¹And Yhwh said to me again, "Go, love a woman loved by a neighbor and an adulteress, like Yhwh's love for the sons of Israel, as they face toward other gods and love raisin cakes."

²So I bought her for myself for fifteen pieces of silver and a homer of barley and a lethech of barley.

³And I said to her, "Many days you will dwell with me. You will not whore and you will not be for a man—indeed, I will be for you."

⁴Because many days the sons of Israel will dwell: no king, no prince, no sacrifice, no pillar, and no ephod or teraphim.

⁵After the sons of Israel turn and seek Yhwh their god, and David their king, they will fear Yhwh and his goodness at the end of days.

A new wife

The main issue in Hosea and the entire Book of the Twelve is faithfulness: faithfulness of Yhwh toward the land and people, and the faithfulness of the land and people toward Yhwh. The latter fails, but the former, never. When the people were unfaithful, the land was a prostitute and the people were adulterers. The faithfulness was inextricably tied to the fate of the land and people. While Yhwh allowed both to prosper, he needed to change their minds, so they understood reality: he provided, is providing, and will provide anything and everything they possessed. To teach this lesson, he would take them both, land and people, into a state where everything was stripped away, and would offer them a word to their understanding. Then the land

and people would become his completely, and they could enjoy his bounty.

The current chapter moves to the next "generation," the addressee of the book. This text begins with an important difference: the people are mentioned but the land is not. Just as the mother was a prostitute, so the children have ended up the same. By promoting the prostitution of their mother, her children were adulteresses and beloved by others, as well. Like mother, like daughter.[1]

If we keep the characters separate in the narrative of chs. 1-3, then we have a second marriage taking place in this chapter. In 1:2b, we read, "Go, take for yourself a woman of whoring and children of whoring, for the land has whored indeed from following Yhwh." The unfaithfulness highlighted in that verse came from the land. She was the one who whored. Chapter 2 depicted the sins of the mother, the land, as they arose because of the children, the people, in order to convince her to stop whoring. In ch. 3, however, the children's unfaithfulness is implicated, as well.

This opens the question as to what sin the people committed. What specifically did the people need to correct? What have they done? The specific ways the people strayed will be addressed throughout the book.

We delve more deeply into the sin of the people. Chapters 1 and 2 primed the reader to understand apostasy to other gods as *the* sin that originates in ignorance. We know that Yhwh would test the people's paternity. Turning to the specific actions of the people, the author began to detail their sin in this chapter as they

---

[1] See Ezek 16:44.

struggled with the trappings of civilization. The Baals and the pageantry of power and religion—those were the distractions Yhwh had to teach them to turn away from.

Commentary

V. 1 The judgement turned from the mother—the land—to the children—the people—because they have been unfaithful. Yhwh told the prophet to "love" a woman here, in the way that he told him to "take" for himself a woman of whoredom in ch. 1. The similarity between the scenes can confuse the reader, who is left wondering if this is a separate event or a retelling of the previous one. The previous chapter implied the people complicity in the land's rebellion, and now the prophet makes it explicit.

Since ch. 2 distinguished between the mother/land and children/people, I read this as a separate event. In ch. 1, Yhwh addressed the unfaithfulness of the *land*, whereas here he states that he is addressing "Yhwh's love for the *sons of Israel*."

We must stay focused on the theme of loyalty, symbolized by marriage. If we interpret too literally, then this chapter sounds incestuous—that is, Yhwh marrying the children of his wife. Note, however, that this verse says the prophet must marry a woman who is an adulteress, not the specific daughter of the unfaithful woman. The people must show perfect loyalty to Yhwh, in the same way a wife must do so with a husband, as the children's mother was to conduct herself with their father.

The phrase "loved by a neighbor" bears multiple meanings through the Bible that work together to underscore her unfaithfulness. This term for "neighbor" carries a legal connotation, as we see in the Ten Commandments: "Do not bear a false testimony against *your neighbor*" (Exod 20:16, emphasis added), and "Do not covet the wife of *your neighbor*" (Exod 20:17b, emphasis added). In those contexts, the term implies someone with whom one has direct contact, maybe on a regular basis. "Loved by a neighbor," therefore, emphasized the individual whom the Ten Commandments requires the reader to respect, not someone with whom one carries out illicit affairs.

The author plays on the consonants of this phrase, "loved by a neighbor," to underscore the wife's wickedness. The consonants for "neighbor," רֵעַ, *rea',* can also be vocalized "evil," רָע, *ra'.* Also, the consonants for "loved by," אֲהֻבַת, *'ahuvat,* can be the feminine form of "lover of" if vocalized differently (אֹהֶבֶת, *'ohevet*). The author thus created a visual pun between "loved by a neighbor" and "lover of evil." Bringing all these connotations together, the people are beloved by those around them—not just visitors, but people they know, which is evil as they continue to be distracted from their husband, Yhwh.

Finally, the people were introduced here as "lovers of raisin cakes." This detail seemed extraneous in that verse, as it could have stopped with "other gods." While the cakes may or may not have been a cultic item in itself, they still could manifest their continuing misunderstanding that Baal, not Yhwh, brought bounty and grain.

V. 2 While the land offered Yhwh's bounty, silver and grain, to woo Baal, in this verse the prophet purchased another prostitute, the people this time, with the same items. Though the woman was not explicitly called a prostitute like the woman in 1:2, the narrator acquired this woman in an exchange. On the one hand, one can read this as a simple commercial transaction: "The price for her was such-and-such, so I paid it." This assumption leads to discussion of how much she was worth, how much grain is worth, etc.

On the other hand, the complex price—silver plus grain—reinforced the themes of sin we see already. Their and their mother's sin has been not to recognize that all things—precious metal and grain—come from Yhwh, not from Baal. The mother followed anyone who produced these good things for her. Precious metal was an expression of trouble in 2:10, where Yhwh multiplied precious metals, but the people made them into Baals. Thus, silver here reiterated one of the main temptations the people had. They acquired wealth and attributed it to their lovers. As a reminder of who brings grain, the narrator offered grain to the unfaithful wife, who loved the raisin cakes of her other lovers. When she was offered silver and grain, she was reminded of where these good things come from, to further the teaching that Yhwh was trying to get through to them.

V. 3 The narrator, now that he has paid, would have her live exclusively with him. This action seems overbearing to the modern reader if we do not read this section in the context of the first two chapters. As a result, we must remain focused on the themes of this book so far, which make crystal clear that she "not be for a man."

Yhwh did not simply want to possess the people but is teaching the people the importance of relying on him exclusively in order to prosper. They lacked loyalty and found trouble when they looked to other men, other fathers, other providers to give them what they wanted and needed, resulting in a cursed land. Their lives would go more smoothly if they remained steadfast with reality, in which only Yhwh does, can, and will provide.

Moreover, Yhwh wanted to ensure the paternity of his children. When he thought he sowed in ch. 1, the children of Baal came up because of his wife's infidelity. The only way to be completely sure that the child would be his is to separate her from any foreign "seed." Yhwh did not want the people's womb or mind filled from some other source besides himself.

V. 4 Yhwh wanted the people free of political and cultic powers besides him. "King" and "prince" represented political powers, and "sacrifice," "pillar," "ephod," and "teraphim," cultic powers. As explained in the introduction, the separation between humans and Yhwh begins with the mindset that humans need to control their own destinies. Human power allows one to protect the necessities and luxuries of life. Sacrifice and pillar are used to cajole and supplicate the deity, in order to manipulate him into giving the necessities and luxuries of life, and ephod and teraphim give humans insight into what the deity will do in the future, to safeguard oneself. All of them work to safeguard humans' safe existence—without Yhwh.

Yhwh wanted to exorcise the idea from them that they have the ability to determine their own fate, so that they might depend exclusively on him. When they would find themselves lacking after chasing other gods, Yhwh's word alone would remain in order to lead them back to the right path.

Furthermore, the scene recalled the people's post-Exodus sojourn in the מדבר, *midbar*, "wilderness," where they depended completely on Yhwh. They had no king or prince, though they did have the other items. Nevertheless, they only had those other items as a result of following the command given to them by Moses. Hence, they were forced to remain true to the word of Yhwh—until they betrayed it and turned to Baal-Peor in

Num 25:1-5. While the time of obedience was short-lived, it remained the paradigm of intimacy between Yhwh and the people of Israel.[2] Hence, this scene tied with 2:16, where Yhwh promised to lure his wife (the land, in that scene) out into the wilderness to win her loyalty back.

V. 5 The people will live for a while without any distraction, dedicated to Yhwh alone. The children resulting from their seclusion could only be his—no paternity test needed. The people will seek only Yhwh as their god, and only the king he provided for them, one who will remain faithful to his god. They will show that they fear Yhwh and will follow his will. These children, though, represent the next generation after the time of the readers.

This will be the "end" of days, when the next David comes. The very end of this epoch of time will be marked when the people learn the will of Yhwh and act accordingly. They will remain faithful and trust in Yhwh's exclusive provision for them, with no "additional assistance" from other gods.

End of fornication, beginning of trust in Yhwh's will

Humans must be separated from any means of provision that their imagination can latch onto if they want to depend on Yhwh. Every human institution offers life, but not one is compatible with the god who gives life. For the people's sake, Yhwh purchases them and takes them away from every imagined source of provision.

Yhwh wants to seclude his wife, ensuring the next generation of children are his. The land, his first wife, fornicated previously with foreign gods, and the children, his second wife, lauded those gods,

---

[2] We can note here the Rabbinic Midrashic tradition of interpreting the Song of Songs—a song of intimate love—as being sung at the crossing of the Red Sea after leaving Egypt (Exod 15). See the ancient Jewish midrashic work, *Song of Songs Rabbah*.

and fornicated with political and religious power. Israel's god will bring the latter back by taking her to where no one can interfere with foreign seed and ideas. For both wife and children, the land and the people, Yhwh describes the perfect location as the מדבר, *midbar*, "wilderness," when the people were and will be sequestered with his word. For the people, this means no leadership, no turning to others to receive good things that only Yhwh can and will provide.

At this point, the reader has seen the entire story of Israel, beginning to end. Yhwh married her, she went astray seeking good things, Yhwh deprived her of good things, and she turned back to him and received good things again so that the next generation can hope to be Yhwh's. This is the pattern that will be elaborated in the rest of Hosea and in the Book of the Twelve.

Chapter 4

¹Hear the word of Yhwh, O sons of Israel, because Yhwh has a dispute with the dwellers of the land, for there is no truth, nor kindness, nor knowledge of God in the land.¹

²Swearing and lying, killing and stealing and adultery—they broke out and blood touched blood.

³Therefore, the land mourns, and every dweller in her languishes. Among the beast of the field, bird of the air, and also fish of the sea, they will be gathered.

⁴Indeed may no one dispute, may no one contend with anyone. Your people are like those who contend with a priest.²

⁵You will fall in the day, and also the prophet will fall with you at night, and I will destroy your mother.

⁶My people are destroyed because of a lack of knowledge because you refused knowledge, so I will refuse you from serving as a priest for me. And you forgot the Torah of your god; I will forget your sons—even I.

⁷As they increased, so they sinned against me. I will turn their glory into shame.

⁸The sin of my people they eat, and to their iniquity they lift up their appetite.

---

¹ The second-person reference in this verse is in the plural.
² The rest of the second-person reference from here to the end of the chapter are in the masculine singular except where noted.

⁹And it will be like people, like priest. I will visit his ways upon him, and his deeds I will return to him.

¹⁰They will eat but not be satisfied, they will whore but not spread, because they gave up paying attention to Yhwh.

¹¹Whoring, wine, and young wine take the heart.

¹²My people will ask of its tree, and their staff will tell them, when a spirit of whoredom caused them to err, and they whored from underneath their gods.

¹³At the tops of the mountains they sacrifice, and on the hills they burn incense, under oak, poplar, and elm, because her shade is good. Therefore, your daughters whore, and your daughters-in-law commit adultery.

¹⁴I will not visit upon your daughters because they whore, or upon your daughters-in-law because they commit adultery. For they separate with the whores, and with the holy women they sacrifice. A people who does not understand will be brought down.

¹⁵If you are a whore, O Israel, let not Judah be ashamed. So do not come to Gilgal, and do not go up to Beth-Aven, and do not swear by the life of Yhwh.³

¹⁶For like a turning cow, Israel has turned. Now Yhwh will shepherd them like a lamb in a large place.

¹⁷Ephraim is bound to idols. Let him rest.

---

[3] In this verse, Israel and Judah are both addressed as masculine singular, but with a second-person plural pronoun in the imprecation against going to Beth-Aven and swearing.

¹⁸ *Their drink has turned, they have indeed whored, they have loved dishonor, her shields.*

¹⁹ *A spirit has bound her in her wings, and they will be ashamed of their sacrifices.*

Explaining the current state

Transitioning from the first three chapters, which set up the context of mother, husband, and children, the original transgression of the land is no longer focal. Now the paternity test begins. Yhwh has begun to examine and judge the people based on how much they resemble him.

While it would be easy to blame Yhwh for the current state of the land and people, this chapter explains that the people's love of sin and ignorance lay at the root. Yhwh began this new section of the text with an accusation against the people. Because the people loved sin, they remained ignorant. They turned from Yhwh and his word in order to live how they wanted, and their situation became miserable. Once they ignored Yhwh's word, they no longer knew how to live properly, in harmony with nature and with each other, so they sank even lower.

The priests served to teach the people. The spirit of Deut 17 is implicit in this chapter. "According to the spoken teaching (lit. *torah*) that they (the priests, the Levites) teach you, and according to the judgment that they tell you, you will do" (Deut 17:11a). Yhwh set up a system so that the people would never stray from Torah: a) the priests would know Torah, b) they would judge the people, and c) the people would obey.

Once the priests left out step (a), though, the people obeyed the ignorant, unjust, unwise judgments of those who were to safeguard Torah. The priest was not the only one judged, but he was called out for special scrutiny. The main role of the priest was teacher, not cultic functionary. The latter makes him a Baalist. Verses 1-3 outline the transgressions of the people in the land, and then vv. 4-19 enumerate the sins of the priest and the cultic manifestations of his incorrect teaching among the people. The people's wicked, harlotous actions originated in a teaching, the self-serving teaching of the priest, which led them to idol-worship, depicted as Baal in the previous chapters.

Turning to Yhwh's Torah, the correct instruction, would resolve the poor situation the sons of Israel found themselves in. His word taught them to submit to him as the sole source of well-being. Contention among the people proved their lack of trust in this instruction, because they fought among themselves to acquire things and look out for themselves. Obedience, therefore, would lead to peace among the people, should they choose it.

The first section, chs. 1-3, highlighted the people's ignorance as the source of their apostasy; Yhwh would have to teach them. In this chapter, Yhwh began to teach them by pointing out the concrete ways in which their ignorance led to their rebellious actions and current misery. Yhwh's priests, tasked as teachers of Torah, stood at the source of the problem because they did not teach the people correctly.

Commentary

V. 1 The new section announces, "Hear the word of Yhwh." In the minds of the sons of Israel they had their own word, their own teaching, their own way of understanding how to live. With the summons "hear," Yhwh would like them to begin to listen to and obey him.

Chapter 4

Yhwh is coming against the people immediately. He brought his contention against them for the wickedness they were spreading through the land: no truth, kindness, or divine knowledge. These were three of the dowry gifts that Yhwh bestowed on his bride, the land. The children should thus possess them, as well, to identify themselves as his.[4] They followed a false word that contradicted his, and so rejected these gifts.

"Truth" was listed first because, as we saw above, misunderstanding where provision came from corrupted everything. Furthermore, this multifaceted word can mean "stability," as in the state of Hezekiah's kingdom in Isa 39:8, and "faithfulness, loyalty," as in Exod 18:21, where it was parallel to "fear of god."

Without truth and faithfulness, the people had no love or "kindness" toward one another. Their incorrect presupposition drove out "knowledge of God" or the teaching of *the* god, Yhwh. He would have to teach them the correct word if they were to display any goodness or kindness in the land.

The people were living according to the word we saw in the first section, in which they, like all human beings, believed that their striving brought them the good things they wanted. When the people did not trust in Yhwh as sole provider, they strove with others to protect their own wealth and to take what they could. Similarly, they had to flatter, cajole, and—if possible—vanquish earthly powers to get the things they wanted. Furthermore, if they followed the word of Baal, they had to acquire gold and grain (by

---

[4] See 2:22-23. This declaration is reminiscent of the episode of Judah and Tamar in Gen 38. When Tamar was about to be punished for her pregnancy, she produced the symbols of Judah to prove that he was the father of her child (Gen 38:25). Perhaps if the children of the land produced the dowry given by Yhwh, they could prove that he is their father.

whatever means) to flatter and cajole the deity. If he did not provide, then they had to get more gold and grain to flatter him more, or to proceed to another god. The word of Baal, the word of earthly wisdom, dictated that they grab and hold on to what they want.

The image of the disobedient land fell away as the text focused on the "sons of Israel" and the "dwellers of the land."[5] The land whored and her dwellers showed who their father was.

V. 2 Whatever the people thought they did correctly, they broke Yhwh's most basic precepts. The prophet enumerated the sins more specifically. Significantly, his vocabulary echoes the words of the Ten Commandments; of the five sins, three of them—murder, theft, and adultery—directly reference them (Exod 20:13, 15, and 14, respectively), by using the very same language. He thus accused them of contradicting the most basic, shortest, and most straightforward of commandments.

The other two sins, swearing and lying, also resonate with Exod 20, as they point to the commandments of "lifting up Yhwh's name for a lie" (Exod 20:7) and the "false testimony" against one's neighbor (Exod 20:16). Even if the "swearing" and "lying" do not tie as closely with the words in Exod 20, the verbatim nature of the following words invites the reader to connect the entire passage to the Ten Commandments. The word of Baal promotes striving against one's neighbor, so using the name of the god to add authority to one's word—even if it is false—and testifying to a lie against one's neighbor aids in getting more for oneself at the expense of the neighbor.

---

[5] "Israel" refers to all the people, although elsewhere the same term connotes the Northern Kingdom when it contrasts with Judah.

Chapter 4

The text applies equally to the reader, who must beware not to absolve him- or herself too quickly from the sins listed. One can quickly and plausibly deny any murder, theft, and adultery, and so be out from under half of the accusations. In one's mind, one is less guilty than the "other people" who are in obvious fact murderers, thieves, and adulterers; one comes out looking not so bad—at least half-virtuous. Such self-righteous thinking pulls one into the trap of contradicting the previous verse; the supreme offense is lack of truth, kindness, and divine knowledge. As a result, the reader's imagined half-virtue is an illusion.

Perhaps readers can tick off a few boxes of correct actions, but they still function according to the word of Baal. They lie in claiming faithfulness to Yhwh's teaching. They still strive for fulfilling their own needs and desires, and they will still sell out their neighbor for their own good rather than give to another for the sake of kindness. They rely only partially on Yhwh to provide for them, and on themselves for the rest. A veneer of piety will not absolve them, because the lie of ignorance still pervades the land.

V. 3 Previously we read how the incorrect actions of the land led to a paternity test for the people, but now we see that the actions of the people caused the land to suffer. In 2:4 Yhwh exhorted the children to "contend" with their mother because of her sin. The children had to bear the correct word to their mother, the land. The present verse claimed that the children caused problems for the land. This juxtaposition strengthens the tie between the suffering of people and of land, and the wide-reaching effects of the people's rebellion. The entire land with its people suffered as a result of these negative activities. The statement may seem exaggerated at first, as one can always find great areas where there is no suffering. The text, therefore, is arguing for a counterintuitive stance, whereby the suffering of the land anywhere can be traced back to the rebellion of the people.

If one assumes the point of view of the text, that of the case Yhwh was arguing, we see the land was suffering. The land languished and did not enjoy the bounty that it could. Yhwh was withholding from the land so that the people might realize the results of their ignorant actions. One can argue some areas were doing well, and some people were getting along well, but this in fact exemplifies the problem: some prospered while others suffered.

The powerful depend on the efforts of their own hands to dam up resources so they can enjoy what they want. These actions leave less for others, creating poor people. If the people did not dam up resources, Yhwh would not deprive the land of good things. The land could provide plenty for every person, but it will not produce until all people understand that taking for themselves at the expense of the poor leaves less to go around.

Humans cannot separate themselves from the languishing in nature that they see, but will be subject to the whims of nature just like an animal. Every dweller in the land will suffer, whether human or animal. The suffering, therefore, is not restricted to the dry land, but to the earth in general. Building a city makes one feel separate from the whims of nature, but humans are just as exposed as any animal, bird, or fish. They will all be gathered together in the mourning land.

V. 4 The people were contending with one another. Whether or not these actions are associated with judicial contention, the people would not live in harmony with each other. They were striving against each other to get what they thought they deserved. Getting and acquiring prevented any communal harmony.

Yhwh addressed the priest rather than the people here when he obliquely accused the people of arguing with the one who was supposed to be teaching them. The addressee changed from a plural in v. 1, in which all the sons of Israel were addressed, to a singular addressee here, likely addressing an authority, named in v. 6 as the priest. He had a responsibility to teach the people Yhwh entrusted to him. By teaching this word to them, the priest offered them the means to pass Yhwh's paternity test. The people ignored Yhwh's word by constantly arguing with each other and the priest. They did not submit to the word; they argued. The religious authority was in charge of making sure they heard and obeyed this message.

V. 5 When the people are contentious, they cause their leaders to suffer and fall. The prophet wanted to ensure that the priest from the previous verse was aware of this. Moreover, the prophet who tries to teach can also become a victim. Those who would contend with the word would just as soon consume its messenger. Without the knowledge of God that was mentioned in v. 1, the people destroy their leaders and would-be teachers.

As the people disobey, the land suffers. This verse preserved the distinct roles of land and people. The mother of the people, the land, would be destroyed as a result of the people's disobedience. Yhwh tested the faithfulness, the trust, of the people, to see who they are loyal to. He does so by withholding the bounty of the land—that is, by no longer providing fineries to his bride. She is broken, and we will see who the children will turn to under duress, which will prove who their father is.

V. 6 This verse is central to the Book of Hosea, as well as the Book of the Twelve, because it starkly explains the link between the condition the people found themselves in and Yhwh's instruction, Torah. The people's destruction could be traced to ignorance of this teaching. They did not know Torah, and so did not have a chance of living or acting correctly, hence depriving the land of truth, kindness, and knowledge of God (4:1).

The priest would be removed because he had not been teaching Yhwh's word. Hebrew links these actions verbally: as the priest *refused* knowledge, so Yhwh *refused* the priest. Torah is the essential role of the priest, so dereliction in this duty sufficed to get him removed. Whereas one may believe that the main role of the priest—ancient or modern—was to perform cultic functions, this verse defined teaching as the principle task. A priest ignorant of Torah lacked the essential ability to fulfill his role.

The next generation, and thus hope for the future, would be forgotten. Another verbal link tied these actions; priests *forgetting* the Torah led to Yhwh *forgetting* the sons. Whether these "sons" were the next generation of priests who would inherit the position (e.g., the sons of Eli in 1 Sam 2), or the people in general in a metaphorical sense (e.g., students as "sons"), Yhwh expressed the end of hope. Without Torah, the people—even the land—could not continue to the next generation.

V. 7 The increase of the people brought more sin as their lack of knowledge of God became more and more problematic. "Increase" here could have two meanings. First, it could mean that they increased in numbers; the more people there were, the more sin there was. Second, it could mean that they increased in substance; as the people gained more wealth, they had more opportunity and reason to sin. The two meanings are not exclusive, so they could have increased both in number and in substance.

More numbers and wealth brought them more self-determination and glory in themselves—the root of their problem. They became smug about their ability to preserve their own livelihoods, and so believed they needed Yhwh less. They were already suffering from ignorance of Torah, and they drifted easily toward the word of Baal, wherein they prospered according to their own influence and guile.

An end is imminent. They cannot prosper truly until Yhwh teaches them not to glory in themselves and in the teaching of Baal, but in Yhwh alone in spite of themselves. Yhwh would help them by—ironically—bringing them to shame, the opposite of glory and self-assuredness.

V. 8 The priests benefited when the people remained ignorant of Torah because sin gave the clergy material wealth. The verse depends on a wordplay in Hebrew. The word חטאת, *xaṭaʾat*, can mean either the act of sinning or the sacrifice associated with atoning for that act. The author played on this double meaning. As the people committed more *sin*, they offered more *sin offerings*, which the priest and his family ate. When the people were ignorant of Torah, they had to offer more sin offerings, providing better meals for the priests' families. We can imagine the priests licking their lips as they saw the sin that aroused their "appetite."[6]

---

[6] The shift in pronouns causes some confusion here. Those who are eating seem to be the priests, plural. In the previous two verses, the third person plural referent is the people, and the singular addressee is the priest. Now the priests are in the third person, rather than the addressee, and plural, rather than singular. The referent must be the priests, because they are the ones to eat the sacrifice, and "my people" functions such that it cannot be the subject.

Furthermore, the final referent is singular, that is, "his appetite," which I translated "their appetite." The priests lifted up their appetite to the iniquity of the people, and so

V. 9 The priest sinned and withheld Torah. The people therefore did not know how to act, so they sinned, which the priest gained from, and the people's sinful actions would eventually consume the priest. Since the priests were in charge of teaching the people, the ways the priests followed would be the ways the people followed. The paternity test of the people commenced, and the land languished for all its inhabitants. The priest would receive the recompense of his ways, there would be disputes among the people, and there would be destruction of the land. The people would suffer alongside their priest.

V. 10 The efforts the people made would not pay off once Yhwh tested them through deprivation. Their food would not be enough to feed them, and as much as they copulated they would not increase in numbers. We cannot reduce the accusation of "whoring" to fleshly relations. While it may refer to engaging in sex among people, apostasy and turning to other gods have been the main action of "whoring" used so far in the Book of Hosea. By remaining ignorant of Yhwh's word, the people's material wealth and physical numbers would stop. The priests deprived them of this word, and so the people could no longer eat and multiply. Lack of Torah meant lack of prosperity.

V. 11 High on their egos, the people lost their ability to think as they indulged in the pleasures of illicit relations and drunkenness. "Wine" and "young wine" referred to the fruits of the land, and "whoring" to apostasy. Just like their mother, their minds were corrupted by too much prosperity and the desire to follow after

---

ate the offering. Perhaps here they lifted up the appetite of the high priest to the iniquity of the people, so that the high priest benefits. While some of the pronominal references are confusing, the priests clearly benefited materially from the sins of the people. The next verse showed that the distinction between the two disappeared when looking toward their fate.

various gods. As I mentioned before, "heart" refers to the seat of reason in the ancient world, not of feelings. Hence, this verse does not mean that their feelings are being taken over, but their reason. So just as being drunk kept them from thinking straight, their desire for prosperity inebriated them further. They could no longer think straight, so Yhwh will need to correct them.

V. 12 Their sense completely left them. Unfaithfulness, the spirit of whoredom, motivated the people to turn to other gods so they could control their own destinies. They turned to divination because they could not stand not to know what was going to happen. The text ridiculed them by depicting them speaking to inanimate objects.[7] Thus the Israelites talking to, let alone supplicating, objects, such as a tree and a staff, revealed true insanity.

The text then immediately accused them of sexual misconduct. One does not need to infer that the people took part in literal sexual acts, because we have seen that this term, "whoredom," refers more often to apostasy in this book. By the desire, even need, to find out the future and control their own destinies, the people committed prostitution by turning to these objects to provide for them.[8]

---

[7] The text is exaggerating for the sake of parody. The people were probably not praying to the object, *per se*. These objects were likely reminders of the "spirit" of the being to which they considered themselves to be praying to. Similarly, someone may put a hand on a Bible and pray with closed eyes in our day. The person is not praying to the book, but to the god imagined to be manifested by the book.

[8] A couple of linguistic ambiguities arise from this verse. First, the phrase "from underneath their gods/god," offers multiple possible interpretations. The last word, אלהיהם, *'elohêhem*, can be translated "their gods" or "their god." Also, "from under" can signify subjugation, as a slave is "under" his master, or it can point to a physical sexual position. Combined together, the people have moved out from under their god, Yhwh, to go under other gods, like the Baals, both for intercourse and for service.

V. 13 The cult to other gods continued among all the people, though the text calls out the daughters and daughters-in-law specifically to display the shame brought on by the entire generation. Families had a duty to teach their children, and families lost this ability and "did not understand" once the priest stopped teaching. The daughters brought shame on their families when they whored. Families with sons bore the shame, as well, because their sons' wives committed adultery. It is not a single group or act that the text accuses. The young women of the next generation were corrupted and brought shame on the older generation who failed teach them.

V. 14 Responsibility for correct teaching and submission to Yhwh lay with the priest first, and the men second. Significantly, the daughters and daughters-in-law will not be punished, even though they brought shame on their families, because others were at fault. Hebrew makes a distinction between feminine verbs and masculine verbs. In the previous verse and the current verse, the verbs for "whore" and "commit adultery" are in the feminine. The verbs for "separate" and "sacrifice" in the current verse, however, are masculine. The masculine actors referred to by the verbs caused of the problem.

The men were leading the women astray, and so bore the punishment. They were the ones who invited the whores to whore, and who sacrificed to other gods with the holy women. Again, we do not need to assume that this verse must refer to sexual intercourse (though the verse does not exclude such an

---

Second, the Hebrew text causes some confusion around referents, but it points to the unfaithfulness of the people. The people are treated as a singular in the first half of the verse and a plural in the second half. One could try to find a different referent for the singular (the plural must be the people), but none is apparent. The people's collective asking advice from a tree results in the distributed acts of harlotry by individuals.

interpretation), as whoring and adultery have pointed to submission to illicit gods so far. Thus the "holy women" do not need to refer to temple prostitutes, but women involved in any way in the cults of other gods.[9]

V. 15 Because of the people's cultic confusion, the prophet commanded them *not* to worship or even evoke Yhwh's name. The people's whoredom caused them to worship in a syncretistic manner, wherein they thought they could go up to any cultic site and call on Yhwh. They think they could appeal to whatever deity they desire. This is the disloyal, self-serving thinking process that makes it impossible for them to dedicate themselves to Yhwh alone.

Yhwh commanded that Judah be spared the whoring of Israel. This was not because Judah was free of this impure worship. While Israel was called the whore, both Judah and Israel were told not to go up to the cultic sites of Beth-Aven and Gilgal, on the northern border of Judah. Moreover, they were not to go there to swear by the life of Yhwh.

V. 16 The relationship between Yhwh and Israel would change so that Yhwh would have to bring them all back together. A cow stands still or lumbers slowly, whereas sheep wander around. Since Israel would no longer stand where they should, they needed to be gathered back in. Because Israel kept turning away from Yhwh, he will shepherd them back to himself as in a pasture.

V. 17 Ephraim will not escape from the idols that he fashioned, and they would demonstrate this fact, given enough time. They

---

[9] The "holy women" could mean priestesses, but we have no way to confirm the function of these individuals. Historically, some commentators translated this word as "cultic prostitutes," but no evidence of such a practice has ever been discovered in Israel.

could not go exclusively to Yhwh because of their tie to the other gods. Their desire to control and provide good things for themselves doomed them to ignorance. So Yhwh let them discover their own destiny and find out what life will be like among those gods they bound themselves to.

V. 18 Being bound to idols in the previous verse meant staying with good things that turned bad and relying on useless things. As wine turns to vinegar, their prosperity was corrupted because of their whoring. They did not choose what brought them honor: respecting marital duty. Rather than depend on Yhwh for defense, they chose their shields.[10] As we will see throughout the Book of the Twelve, when Yhwh decides to allow forces to attack, no human shields can defend against them.

V. 19 Their deepest core motivated them to commit apostasy. In biblical physiology, the "spirit" is the breath that gives life; when one has no more breath, one is no longer alive. Furthermore, the spirit one has motivates that person to act in a particular way. If one has a good spirit, one acts in a good way; if one has a bad spirit, one acts in a bad way. Thus, a spirit can be linked to a teaching. A good teaching can give a good spirit, which will motivate a person to act correctly. The spirit of a god allows one to act according to the god's will and teaching. When the people act according to Yhwh's will, they have the "spirit of Yhwh," and when they act according to Baal's will, they have the "spirit of Baal."

The spirit of whoredom has caught them up and will doom them, just as a strong wind can completely disrupt the flight of a bird. In addition to an "animating force" or "spirit," *ruax* can

---

[10] The referent of "her" here is not entirely clear, but it might most easily refer to Ephraim in v. 17.

mean a wind. As a strong wind forces a bird to fold up its wings to avoid injury, so the spirit of individual fears and desires caught up to Ephraim. This spirit caused them to act in the way they do, striving to benefit themselves, to supplicate any god who will listen. They would not be loyal to Yhwh. In the end, the sacrifices they performed to all of these gods for their own gain, and at the expense of others, would cause them shame.

Nature abhors a vacuum

When the priests did not teach the Torah of Yhwh to the people, another teaching came in to take its place. All living things breathe, animated by their spirit; without spirit—the same as "breath" in Hebrew—the creature dies. One spirit or another was functioning in the body of Israel. The self-serving inactivity of the priests denied them the good spirit, the spirit of Yhwh, and so invited a wicked spirit of apostasy. Ephraim was therefore bound to idols, and the people performed shameful actions.

Everyone was filled with this spirit of Baal, but this judgment placed responsibility for communal wrongdoing at the feet of those in power. Once the priest taught, the men had a responsibility to conduct themselves correctly. If the men stray, though, they bring the women down with them. Yet no one was innocent. Even though the priests taught incorrectly, the men were culpable for their incorrect actions. The women were called harlots, even though they were following the men. All were guilty, but more accountability rests higher up in the hierarchy.

The reader/hearer of this book must take notice, but especially the teachers and the priests. Yhwh focused on teaching, and cultic activity is never lauded in this chapter. Those with authority must cling that much more stubbornly to Yhwh's teaching. Hearing this word from the mouth of the prophet and priest is the cure for the selfish, self-rewarding teaching of Baal. Listening to one's own intuitions and ignoring Yhwh's word will only lead to selfish cultic service at the expense of others. The natural consequence of relying on oneself is that the sources one seeks out for good things will eventually dry up. Only Yhwh's interventions will continue the flow. The correct approach is to accept reality: Yhwh is the only source of all things, good and bad. One cannot preserve the good or prevent the bad by oneself, or with the aid of a malleable god—just another manifestation of one's self.

Chapter 5

¹Hear this, O Priests, and pay attention, O House of Israel; and House of the King, give ear! For the judgment is for you. For you became a trap at Mizpah and a spread-open net against Tabor.

²Rebels deepened slaughter, and I am discipline for all of them.

³I know Ephraim, and Israel is not made foreign from me, for now you made others to whore, O Ephraim, and Israel became unclean.

⁴Their deeds will not allow them to return to their god, because a spirit of harlotry is within them and they do not know Yhwh.

⁵The beauty of Israel answered to his face. Israel and Ephraim stumble in their iniquity. Even Judah stumbled with them.

⁶With their flock and their cattle they go to seek Yhwh, but they do not find him. He has withdrawn from them.

⁷Against Yhwh they acted treacherously when they bore foreign sons. Now a New Moon will devour them with their portions.

⁸Blow the horn in Gibeah and the trumpet in Ramah. Call aloud, Beth-Aven, after you, Benjamin!

⁹Ephraim will become a destruction on the day of rebuke. Among the tribes of Israel, I have made known what is lasting.

¹⁰The princes of Judah were like movers of the boundary. Upon them I will pour out my wrath like water.

¹¹Ephraim is oppressed, judgment is broken, when he desired to walk after the commandment.

¹²And I am like the moth for Ephraim and like rot for the House of Judah.

¹³And Ephraim saw his sickness, and Judah his wound; Ephraim went to Assyria and sent to King Jareb. But he is not able to heal you, and he will not heal a wound from you.

¹⁴For I am like the lion to Ephraim, and like the young lion to the house of Judah! I myself, I will tear and I will go! I will bear it and there is no savior!

¹⁵I will go and return to my place until they are ashamed and seek my face. When they have an affliction, they will seek me early.

Reconfiguring apostasy

Reading Hos 5 in light of the first four chapters forces us to read the sin and rebellion of the people specifically as apostasy. The god they followed was the god of whatever teaching they followed. When the people acted in a way contrary to Yhwh's Torah, therefore, we are to see them as not simply disobedient, but disloyal, rejecting Yhwh, and functionally making him no longer their god. It is like a son who disobeys his father. When the father declares, "You are no longer my son!" the father is not making something true by his word, but stating the fact that the father *became* not a father to him once the child no longer acted like his son. Yhwh ceased to be the god of Israel when Israel did not act according to his word. They followed another god, and that god is a Baal; they are sons of Baal.

The chapter emphasizes judgment, specifically against the priests, royal house, and people through oblique references to locations and events from elsewhere in the Bible. Specifically, Hos 5:1 refers to Mizpah, and 5:8 to Gibeah. These locations, in the whole of the Hebrew Bible, encapsulate what is wrong with the rulers of Israel, and the people who follow them with gusto.

In order to understand this chapter, therefore, we must first grasp the intertextual references to apostasy and disobedience that led to violence. We cannot know for certain if references to Mizpah and Gibeah indicate historical events. We do know for certain, however, that these places occur elsewhere in scripture, especially in narratives about apostasy and violence. By delving into those other texts, Hosea's point emerges more conspicuously.

Mizpah, Gibeah, and violence: Judges 19-21

Mizpah and Gibeah function as a location of sin in Judg 19-21, which recounts the terrible crime of the Gibeahites in Benjamin against a Levite's concubine, and Israel's violent reaction against them.[1] When the Levite with his concubine arrived at Gibeah, he could not find hospitality, even when he was willing to provide his own food and animal fodder. An old man brought him in, but immediately after, the townspeople wanted to "know" and violate the guests. The Levite turned over his concubine to the townspeople, who abused her to death. The author depicted

---

[1] The crime of Gibeah paralleled that of Sodom (Gen 19) in significant ways, where the men of Sodom wanted to abuse the guests of Lot. The author of Judg 19-21 thus heightened the severity of the sin of Gideon by drawing a parallel with the archetypal sinful city, Sodom.

Gibeah in a way that could not be worse: victimizing a Levite and fellow-Israelite with lack of hospitality, rape, and murder.

Mizpah moved to center stage for the reckoning against Benjamin in Judg 20. All of Israel met there to plan their next actions against this unambiguously evil action. When the Benjaminites would not surrender, the rest of Israel went to war against them. Israel lost two battles, but they won the final one decisively. Yhwh promised in 20:28 that he would deliver Benjamin into their hand, and did so in 20:35, after the death of 25,100 Benjaminites. Yet the Israelites overstepped their mandate to manifest Yhwh's justice.

This near genocide did not suffice for them. At the end of the chapter, in v. 46, the text repeats that 25,000 Benjaminites were dead. Even then, the Israelites proceeded to attack every Benjaminite city, burn them, and kill every man and beast (20:48). Yhwh delivered Benjamin into their hands, yet they continued their violence to decimate the entire tribe. Mizpah was the staging ground for a nearly complete fratricidal genocide, because the justice that began there turned to revenge and extermination after Benjamin had already been given over to them.

Israel returned to Mizpah to solidify the next step in their strategy of genocide. In the very next chapter (Judg 21), they swore there not to give their daughters to wed Benjaminites, to cut off the tribe from the sons of Israel. Furthermore, the children of Israel condemned to death anyone in their midst who did not fight against Benjamin (21:5). After decimating Benjamin, Israel could not contribute to restoring them, sealing their genocidal fate.

Violence against Benjamin was not enough, so Israel directed their bloodlust inwards. They somehow felt bad about the near-extinction of Benjamin, so they, surprisingly, decided to offer women to them so Benjamin could sire children (21:6). This left them in a pickle: they wanted to give women to Benjamin, but they had sworn not to give any of their women to the Benjaminites (21:7). The "solution" was to find a tribe in Israel who did not go up to fight against Benjamin, and they did so: the inhabitants of Jabesh-Gilead (21:8). The people of Jabesh-Gilead were already condemned to death from the Israelites' first oath, so they provided an outlet for further violence from Israel: the latter killed all the men and all the married women of Jabesh-Gilead and gave the virgins to the remnant of Benjamin. Thus, they technically avoided the ramifications of the second oath by *forcing* these virgins to go to the Benjaminites, because the fathers of these virgins did not voluntarily give their daughters to Benjamin (21:14).

In order to make up for the overwhelming violence against Benjamin that was conceived at Mizpah, and to fulfill the rash oaths they made at the same place, they committed violence precisely against the one tribe who did not commit violence. Every act of violence led to another one, justified (in their minds) by the need to uphold their oaths. It is on this sharp note that the Book of Judges ends.

When Hos 5 references Mizpah, then, the text draws intertextually from the meaning of this place, which represents the corruption of human justice that ignores mercy and kindness. This episode brings evidence of what Hos 4:1-2 accused the people of: lacking mercy and kindness. Moreover, Mizpah intersected some of the actions of Jezreel outlined in my discussion of Hos 1. At Jezreel, Jehu was to remove the current royal house.

The "prophet" gave license to commit even more acts of carnage, which Jehu seemed happy to take on. At Mizpah, the Israelites received from a Levite a command to enact justice, which they extended to self-righteous genocide. In both cases, those entrusted with a duty were puffed up so that they furthered their power through extreme violence.

Apostasy by idol and king: Mizpah in 1 Samuel 7-10

The spotlight of apostasy shone again on Mizpah in 1 Sam 7-10. In the Judg 19-21 story, the people assembled at Mizpah both for war and for pronouncing self-serving, violent oaths. In this 1 Samuel passage, Mizpah fulfilled a cultic function, but associated with judgment and repentance. At Mizpah the people repented from worshiping idols at one point, but later at that same place ironically begged for a king rather than trust in Yhwh.

Yhwh had to convince the people, under intermittent attacks by the Philistines, to abandon their gods and turn to him if they wanted to live. They did so at Mizpah (1 Sam 4-7). It took a military defeat, nevertheless, to bring them to repentance. Despite bringing the Ark of the Covenant with them to Ebenezer from Shiloh, the Israelites lost to the Philistines, who captured it and took it away. The Philistines did not want to keep it, so they gave it back, but this was not enough for Israel to beat their enemies. Possessing the talisman of their Ark could not replace loyalty. Only after the sons of Israel came to Mizpah to repent for worshiping Baals and Asherahs did they beat back the Philistines.

The people rejected Yhwh immediately after this event, however, and Samuel brought them back to Mizpah to reprimand them (1 Sam 7:5-6). Samuel attempted to rule the people by setting up his sons as judges, but they were corrupt, prompting the people to look for different leadership. They asked Samuel for a king, ignorantly rejecting divine protection for human rule, even after they defeated the Philistines without a king. Yhwh, though, explained the big picture to Samuel in response to the people's request: "They have not rejected you (Samuel), but they have rejected me, that I should not reign over them" (1 Sam 8:7).

In 1 Sam 9, Samuel found Saul, a native of Gibeah, to be the first king, and soon after reprimanded the people for rejecting Yhwh and choosing a king (1 Sam 10:17-19).[2] The reprimand took place at Mizpah, further associating this site with apostasy and repentance, but instead of rejecting Yhwh for the Baals and Asherahs, they turned to a king to defend them. There are two ways to reject Yhwh—to turn toward other gods to control nature and toward a king to control the military—and at Mizpah the people of Israel realized both in 1 Samuel. Turning away from Baals, while turning towards a king, returned them to the same place.

Hosea did not simply mention two locations, Gibeah and Mizpah, but deliberately alluded to scriptural events that centered around these locations. Both places connoted apostasy. At the same time, they connected apostasy equally to perversion of justice, worshiping Baals, and longing for human power. In the previous chapter Yhwh was looking for truth (faithfulness), kindness, and knowledge of God. They were not simply missing, Hosea asserts, but the opposite traits had taken over the land.

---

[2] Hence Saul was a surviving Benjaminite. In both Judges and 1 Samuel, the residents of Gibeah are called "sons of Belial" (Judg 19:22 and 1 Sam 10:27). The first crime was wanting to abuse the sojourner; the second crime was to refuse to recognize the king and his entourage. Saul thus bore his hometown's reputation of disobedience, foreshadowing his own fall.

Further defining apostasy

This contextualization of sin shows that disobedience of one towards another does not function on its own, but changes the relationship altogether. The prophet referred to Mizpah to open the chapter—the place highlighted the deep corruption of Israel in its dealings with Yhwh. The fratricide, idol-worship, and desire for a king associated with that place, as well as the egregious crime and first king from Gibeah, all constituted apostasy. Extreme violence, reliance on other gods, and desire for a military leader prove that they worship power, not Yhwh.

While people turn from Yhwh, he provides all that humans might want, though they might want them delivered in a different way. They want to defeat their enemies, avenge wrongs, and receive bounty on their schedule, their terms. If Yhwh does not deliver, they will look elsewhere—but it is not possible to look elsewhere while credibly professing allegiance to Yhwh.

Commentary

V. 1 Judgment came against the priests, people, and king because of their collusion to commit apostasy. The prophet addressed the priests, people, and royal house, which seems redundant, as one could address "O Israel" and include the same people. We saw part of this mechanism in the previous chapter: the priest withholds Torah, and the people sin. In this verse, the person of the king entered the equation. The king became a manifestation of their apostasy, the leader they chose over Yhwh, specifically at Mizpah. The mutual support of all three of these groups of people justified the apostasy—the "trap"—that characterized Mizpah.

Tabor, alongside Mizpah, ties loosely into this same narrative. The object of apostasy, the new king, Saul, met the prophets in the plain of Tabor, when he was first chosen (1 Sam 10:3). At Tabor, therefore, the ill-conceived reign of the first king of Israel began.

V. 2 Slaughter, with its cultic and military meanings, unites the various disloyal actions characterized by Mizpah. The cultic place requires slaughter for animal sacrifice, which often characterizes an oath. Violence against people in wartime exemplifies slaughter, as well. The people's obsession with other gods, to whom they sacrificed, and their obsession with military power, with which they committed slaughter, revealed their rebellion.

Yhwh cannot be separated from his judgment. This aspect of Yhwh was introduced in ch. 4, where Yhwh warned them that he will destroy them. This is not obliteration, for the result of the destruction will be instruction. The rebels would learn about the evil of their slaughter when Yhwh removed from them bounty and earthly safety.

V. 3 Ephraim also committed whoredom in the person of its first king, Jeroboam. We must not forget the link between whoredom and apostasy, established in chs. 1-2. While this verse in Hosea only mentions the land of Ephraim, and not the king or the act itself, we read elsewhere that Ephraim led the people in the worst acts of apostasy. The tribes, in their ambition, spread unfaithfulness throughout the people. Ephraim represents here the initial formation of the Northern Kingdom, which separated from the House of David after the death of King Solomon (1 Kgs 12:16-20). King Jeroboam, who led the rebellion, followed a trend that is already revealed in Hosea's narrative so far.

Jeroboam, an Ephraimite (1 Kgs 11:26), came to rule and misled the Northern Kingdom of ten tribes. King Solomon appointed Jeroboam over all of the region of Joseph (Ephraim and

Manasseh) (1 Kgs 11:28), and shortly after, rebellion broke out. The prophet Ahijah told Jeroboam that he would possess the ten Northern Tribes (1 Kgs 11:26-37). When the son of Solomon, Rehoboam, decided to oppress the people, Jeroboam led Israel in a just rebellion against him (1 Kgs 12:16-19).

Human justice, though, corrupts itself immediately. After the rift with the house of David, King Jeroboam did not pause to commit apostasy in Ephraim: "Then the king took counsel, and made two calves of gold, and said unto them, 'It is too much for you to go up to Jerusalem. Behold your gods, O Israel, which brought you up out of the land of Egypt'" (1 Kgs 12:28). In this way, King Jeroboam abused the authority bestowed on him by the prophet and so followed the archetypal apostasy of Aaron in Exod 32:4. He did not follow the teaching of Yhwh, and so led the people to apostasy. In this way, "Israel became unclean."

V. 4 Behavior begets similar behavior. The "spirit" is the force that animates life, and different spirits animate beings to live in different ways. The people's whoring deeds implied a spirit of whoring as their motivation. If their animating spirit was one of whoring, how could they produce any works reflecting Yhwh's spirit, unless that spirit is replaced by a spirit of faithfulness?

The whoring of Ephraim established that there could not be truth/faithfulness or knowledge of God in the land. In the present verse the prophet explicitly accused the people of not knowing Yhwh. While they may have been eager to profess their knowledge of Yhwh, their actions contradicted their words. Knowledge of Yhwh therefore cannot be solely knowledge in one's mind. If actions do not manifest the knowledge, the knowledge does not function. When the spirit of whoring animates the people, there can be no correct action or knowledge of Yhwh.

V. 5 The beauty (also translated as "pride") given to Israel by Yhwh was misused to seduce other gods. Yhwh wanted her to be beautiful, but a spirit of whoring corrupted her by unfaithfulness and apostasy. Israel and Ephraim thus stumbled in the "iniquity" of their unfaithfulness, and Judah stumbled, as well.

V. 6 Steeped in their wealth, the people could not reach Yhwh, as the teaching was corrupt. The people focused on their possessions to direct themselves to obey Yhwh, rather than examine their actions. The author is making fun of the importance of soothsaying because sacrifice in the ancient world offered answers to questions, as one read the shape of animals' organs for knowledge about the will of a god. Mays suggests that the "seeking" is not a desire to reconnect to their god, but inquiry through cultic means. Whether they look to the riches of their flock or the animals' internal organs for answers, the people look to their possessions to obtain knowledge.[3]

Yhwh then told the people they would not find him. As we learned in Hos 4, one finds Yhwh's will in his Torah. When the people followed Torah, things went well for them. Their actions displayed their impertinence and disrespect. When they did not get what they want, they asked Yhwh what the matter was, rather than remain obedient to his teaching. They assumed something is wrong, and so looked to soothsaying instead of Torah for answers about what the matter might be. From the people's point of view, Yhwh effectively removed himself and would not answer their questions.

V. 7 The cultic rites the people performed would be their undoing. When the bride Israel copulated with the foreign gods,

---

[3] James Luther Mays, *Hosea: A Commentary*, The Old Testament Library (Philadelphia: Westminster Press, 1969), 84.

she bore children for them. As we saw in ch. 2, Yhwh granted his wife beauty, and she used it to bear other men's children. When the people used their bounty to celebrate cultic festivals, their celebration was corrupted by unfaithfulness. No matter what they did in their cult, it could not be for Yhwh because of their persistent ignorance of what Yhwh did for them and expected of them. Each celebration revealed more and more of their ignorance and spirit of whoredom, which led them to the inevitable end of devastation and lack of bounty.

A New Moon will devour them. An ambiguity exists in the phrase "New Moon." On the one hand, it can refer to a monthly festival. On the other hand, it can mean a one-month period of time. I am favoring the former interpretation here, because of the theme of the cult throughout the book so far. Hence, their focus on rites and festivals was the root of their undoing.

The alternate reading implies that it would take only one month to destroy the people and their substance. A swift judgment was coming. We can preserve the ambiguity and bring the meanings together: the corrupt, self-serving cult of the people would bring a swift judgment. Rather than look forward to the next New Moon festival, they should be counting down the days to their end.

V. 8 The horn and trumpet signified a call to arms in this verse, as the text alludes to the fratricidal war of Benjamin in Judges. Benjamin was called out specifically to fight. Moreover, the call to arms went out in Gibeah and Ramah, both in Benjamin, a further reference to the fratricidal war.[4] The previous apostasy and fratricide were catching up to the people.

The previous verse (Hos 5:7) highlights the people's apostasy in their cult, and the following verse presents Ephraim finally being destroyed (5:9), placing this verse in the context between apostasy and destruction. The war with Benjamin unites these two themes. Even though Israel came out against Benjamin for reasons of justice, Israel followed other teachings, and so other gods, and loyalty to the incorrect teaching would destroy them.

Mays, however, states that it is "widely accepted" that this verse relates not to the Israel-Benjaminite war, but to the Syro-Ephraimite war, described in 2 Kgs 15-16, wherein Aram and Ephraim turned against Judah.[5] In 2 Kgs 16, King Pekah of the Northern Kingdom united with the king of Syria to attack King Ahaz, king of Jerusalem and Judah.[6] Ephraim thus condemned themselves doubly by first aligning with an enemy king who did not follow Yhwh, and second, by attacking a brother.

Several dark consequences cascaded from this event. King Ahaz of Judah turned to Assyria for help, and consequently took up Assyrian cultic practices and rearranged the Jerusalem temple to accommodate them (2 Kgs 16:7-18). Assyria invaded the Northern Kingdom, conquered them, and established a new king there, Hoshea. Under the Assyrians, King Hoshea acted like a friend of the empire, but then betrayed his overlords when he wooed Egypt behind their backs (2 Kgs 17:3-4). At that point, Assyria engaged them in a full-on attack, deporting all of Samaria

---

[4] Ramah sits right next to Gibeah and was another option besides Gibeah for the Levite with his concubine to spend the night (Judg 19:11-15).

[5] Mays, *Hosea*, 88-89.

[6] See my notes on 12:3.

for their disloyalty to them, though the biblical narrator stated that they were deported because of disloyalty to Yhwh in many forms (2 Kgs 17:5-23).

Whether the reference is to the Benjaminite or the Syro-Ephraimite war, the idea of corruption in the land is the same. Both display human justice that is rotten to the point of fratricide. Whether Israel went out to destroy their brother, Benjamin, or against their other brother, Judah, the Northern Kingdom looked after itself through so-called justice and self-preservation. Israel did not trust in Yhwh as their only source of life and protection—*twice.*

V. 9 Yhwh taught the people the correct way to act. They knew what was "lasting" or established. In a parallel to Benjamin's destruction, Ephraim would in turn be destroyed because of the apostasy of Jeroboam (1 Kgs 12), as I explained above in v. 3, or because of the apostasy of Ahaz, King of Judah, during the Syro-Ephraimite War (2 Kgs 16:7-18), which I mentioned in v. 8. Yhwh continued to build his case that these children do not act like his children.[7]

V. 10 Greed, motivated by self-preservation, pushes one to take advantage of others' weaknesses to gain more. The "mover of the boundary" thus represented a scoundrel who stole land and betrayed a lack of trust that his land would suffice. Judah was the first tribe to attack Benjamin, at Yhwh's command (Judg 20:18). In the end, as we saw, Israel almost ended up destroying Benjamin completely. Yhwh gave them a command, and they

---

[7] A potential wordplay exists in the word בשבטי, *BŠBṬY*. I translated it here as "among the tribes of." Revocalized, the same consonants could be read, "with my staffs," rendering this phrase as, "With my staffs I made known to Israel what is lasting." The wordplay reveals not only where but how Yhwh will make this information known.

Chapter 5

metaphorically moved his "boundary," and turned justice into genocide. This near-obliteration reframed the aggression of Israel against Benjamin as a basic sin mentioned in the Torah (Deut 27:17) and in Proverbs (Prov 22:28; 23:10; 23:11).

Similarly, when the Syro-Ephraimite coalition attacked Judah, the latter's King Ahaz turned quickly to Assyria to protect his country, even offering treasures from the temple to the foreign king. If this was not enough, he was impressed by the altar at Damascus, and recreated it in Jerusalem. The text there denounces him because he renovated the temple "out of respect to the king of Assyria" (2 Kgs 16:18). Judah invited foreign kings and gods into their territory, their city, and even their temple, respecting these powers to the neglect of Yhwh.

V. 11 Ephraim's spirit was so corrupt because his rebellion and ignorance oppressed him. Even when he attempted to fulfill the commandment, he could not. He had traveled so far down the path toward apostasy that he could not turn back.

The word for "commandment" here looks different than in most places, which suggests a nuanced interpretation.[8] The word used in this verse we also find in Isa 28:10 and 13. That chapter describes the ignorance of the priests, whom the narrator compares to drunks. Since the priests lacked understanding, they commanded the people willy-nilly, with "petty orders," and render Yhwh's commandments unrecognizable. The word for these "petty orders" is the same word used here in Hosea. Hence, we can interpret the "commandments" in this chapter as petty, misconstrued orders. When Ephraim tried to walk after these *so-called* commandments, they "broke judgment." They followed the

---

[8] The more common word for commandment is צוה, *tsivvâ*, whereas here it is צו, *tsav*, missing the final ה-, *-â(h)*. The clear difference in spelling raises the question.

broken, unimportant commandments of cultic service, rather than the true commandment of loyalty.

Once the incorrect teaching has taken over, religious devotion leads to oppression as adherents believe they are doing the right thing. These are the "commandments" mentioned here—they seem like commandments, but they are simply religious "busy work" that cannot produce the desired outcome. The fear of calamity because of falling behind on sacrifices, or getting in bad graces with the divine, prompts people to count on themselves more, instead of cleaving to Yhwh's teaching of submission to his will and חסד, *xesed*, towards others.

V. 12 Yhwh declared—counterintuitively—that he himself destroyed Ephraim and Israel from the inside. We have seen many options for what has caused the corruption among the people: their corrupt spirit (v. 11), treachery (v. 7), iniquity (v. 5), and their deeds and spirit of whoredom (v. 4). Yet Yhwh forced the reader to interpret him as the agent of their degradation. Yhwh's judgment against these attitudes and the actions they engender ate away at them from the inside, and once the rotten core is gone, a correct teaching may take its place.

His word, his teaching, still existed in their midst as a judgment of destruction. In this way, Yhwh inserted himself as the agent of all that the people experience—good and bad. Just as the people needed to learn that Yhwh offered them his bounty, even when they thought it was Baal (2:10), he imposed on them the narrative that he caused their fall, as well. They would have to see their internal corruption as Yhwh's judgment. As a result, the people must submit completely to him in every aspect. Lack of submission initiated their problems; only submission will bring them back.

V. 13 The people looked to kings and earthly powers to provide for them, instead of looking to Yhwh. If the people understood that Yhwh stood at the center of their rot, they would have gone to him for healing. As Ephraim and Judah saw themselves rotting from the inside, they turned to a great foreign king who might contend with Yhwh or make himself great. Earthly power impressed them, not Yhwh, and so they chose an Assyrian king. They would look anywhere except to their own disobedience, the source of their internal rot, or to Yhwh, who caused the rot to happen.

"King Jareb" does not appear in any Assyrian annals that we know. The name "Jareb," though, means either "May he contend" or "He becomes great." The name generically refers to a self-important king—any king, in fact. We could, therefore, translate this phrase as "a great king" or "a king who becomes great."

V. 14 Throughout this chapter, Israel and Judah have been looking for solutions, and here Yhwh revealed that he alone could save the people from their problems. They were the cause of their own problems, because they were ignorant of Yhwh and his teaching as the source of everything, good and bad. Yhwh would teach them by afflicting them. Reflecting similar sentiments to v. 12, this verse expressed how Yhwh was the cause of the destruction among the people. Since the people did not know that Yhwh was the source of their blessings, he would show them by taking away their prosperity. The difference between this verse and v. 12 lay in Yhwh's actions: in v. 12 he slowly destroys by decay; in v. 14, he destroys immediately and violently. Both images identify Yhwh as their ravager.

V. 15 The people would have to come to Yhwh for help when they are "ashamed" and "afflicted." Yhwh was producing a situation where such reactions were inevitable. After he destroyed, Yhwh would return to his place, waiting for the people to turn to him. He hoped for one result: that the people would come to him for help and as the source of good. They could choose to go to their Baal and their human king, following an entrenched, false teaching, or reject the teaching that caused their destruction and turn to him. When they realized what they were doing wrong, they would come to him and his teaching for his help.

The fruit of apostasy

This chapter posits that the evil experienced by the community arose from apostasy. To argue this point, the author must work to convince the reader of a less intuitive definition of apostasy. One may think that apostasy is confined to the formal realm of worship and the cult. In fact, looking for a provider other than Yhwh in any circumstance constitutes apostasy.

By corollary, Hosea redefines what faithfulness is. Committing the correct cultic actions does not constitute faithfulness, but loyalty in all actions. Since Yhwh could not function separately from his teaching, his Torah, betrayal of Torah not only implied betrayal of Yhwh but was the same as betraying Yhwh. Since Torah declared Yhwh as the provider of all things, faithfulness imposes Yhwh as one's only provider. Actively seeking gain outside of Yhwh's provision was apostasy and unfaithfulness.

Faithfulness to this teaching fosters peace in Israel, and disobedience begets violence. This chapter alluded to famous biblical passages wherein Israel suffered because of their ambition. Seeking revenge against Benjamin betrayed Yhwh and Torah, so the consequences came as judgment from Yhwh and Torah; the seed of Yhwh ending the Kingdom of Israel found root in the apostasy from Yhwh and Torah when they had desired a king. In building this intertextual case, Hosea explained how Yhwh was the "moth," "rot," and "lion" who devoured Israel from both the inside and outside. Israel could not exterminate or eliminate this threat, so they had to take mitigating action immediately.

Chapter 6

¹ *"Go, let's return to Yhwh, because he tore, and he will heal us. He strikes, and he binds us up.*

² *"After two days he gives us life, the third day he raises us up, that we might live before him.*

³ *"That we might know, let us pursue knowing Yhwh. His place is established like the morning, and will come like rain to us, like the latter rain casts on the land."*

⁴ What will I do for you, O Ephraim? What will I do for you, O Judah? Your kindness is like the cloud of the morning. Like the dew of the early morning it goes away.[1]

⁵ For this reason, I hewed them by the prophets; I killed them by the words of my mouth, and your judgments are a light that goes forth.[2]

⁶ For I have desired kindness and not sacrifice, and knowledge of God more than burnt offerings.

⁷ For they like Adam transgressed the covenant. There they rebelled against me.

---

[1] The addresses to Ephraim and Judah are in the second-person masculine, but "your kindness" uses a plural possessive. Thus, Yhwh addresses each tribe individually via the prophet, but accuses them of the same transgression.

[2] "Your judgments" uses a singular masculine possessive pronoun, and so the speaker likely addresses someone other than the collective of Israel, which was in the plural in v. 4. Yhwh is addressing the prophet here, as he began in the third person at the beginning of the verse. The tool that comes against the people is the judgment by the word given to the prophet.

⁸Gilead is a city of workers of iniquity; they are supplanted by blood.

⁹And as a band of robbers wait for a man is the group of priests; they murder on the way to Shechem, because they have committed iniquity.

¹⁰In the house of Israel, I have seen horrible things. There harlotry belongs to Ephraim and Israel is polluted.

¹¹Even Judah—he has set a harvest for you, when I restore the captivity of my people.

Recurring apostasy

Yhwh had no reason to trust the people anymore even (especially?) when they constantly paid him lip service. After the threats against the people in ch. 5, the people seemed to want to return to Yhwh—but would they remain true to their word? Even if they believed that they would return to Yhwh, they did not understand what that entails.

Repentance could not come from the same mindset as before, because they did not even know that they strayed from Yhwh until destruction came upon them. They understood only the language of destruction, not the teaching that Yhwh gave them. In ch. 2, they thought their bounty came from various gods. Yhwh had to deprive them so that they might understand that the bounty came only from him. "Repentance" in their minds meant returning to the most successful provider of prosperity. In fact, Yhwh was the only provider—not one choice among many, but the only choice available. It was not enough to turn away from their Baal; the word had to be removed from their vocabulary (2:18). So, when the people said, "Let us return," it meant what they thought it meant until their minds were completely changed.

Their so-called repentance could not last. They based their change of mind on Yhwh's destruction, not on his Torah. Their "repentance" may appear for a moment, but it would disappear as soon as a new deity crossed their path, just like a harlot's devotion toward her lover. She may "fall" for a man, but only until she "falls" again for another one. She follows the one who provides for her—or, better, whom she believed provides for her. If they wanted to change their pull to apostasy, they would have to take Yhwh's Torah to heart.

A key verse, 6:6, juxtaposes what the people give and what Yhwh wants. He will judge how the people live their lives, not whether they "checked off" this or that pious action. The people fooled themselves, with the help of the priests, into thinking that Yhwh wanted offerings, when he wanted complete obedience, manifesting his knowledge through חסד, *xesed,* "kindness." They actually believed in their own actions, that they somehow indicated devotion. Sacrifice did not represent their devotion but contradicted it.

In this chapter, Yhwh rebuked the people because of their immature desire to repent, because they did not know what it meant to turn back to Yhwh. Their desire for repentance did not constitute a true change of ways because they still ignored the word of Yhwh's prophet. He demanded a change of heart—though he may not have expected it would ever transpire.

Commentary

V. 1 The people understood, at least, that Yhwh was the one who struck and tore them, and that he could heal their wounds, as well.

These words are encouraging, reflecting comprehension of Yhwh's power. His power, as we saw last chapter, encompassed harm and healing, destruction and creation.

V. 2 The people affirmed that Yhwh was the one who gave them and continued to give them life. They believed that their life was dedicated to him as they lived "before him." Their fate—good and bad—lay completely in his hands.

V. 3 The people's words were correct in their praise of Yhwh. They lived—that is, were given life—so that they might pursue knowledge of Yhwh. Yhwh reigned over everything, even the morning and the rain, and he gave life to the land. Yhwh was the lone provider.

V. 4 While their words of faith sounded like trust in their god, Yhwh did not believe them. Their strong sentiment was not founded in his teaching. In a metaphorical irony, Yhwh turned their words back on them. While the people identified Yhwh with the rains that brought forth life from the land, Yhwh compared the people to the morning dew that does not water anything, but simply disappears. Their love and trust in Yhwh evaporate easily. While Yhwh heard their words as חסד, *xesed*, the sentiment would not last. Yhwh was still testing whether the people were the children of their mother, a known faithless harlot, and one of her lovers, Baal. They may submit to Yhwh, but when their so-called dedication evaporates, they would fail the test as they move to the next so-called provider.

V. 5 The people fundamentally misunderstood their own faithlessness. They thought the problem was that they strayed. The people were clearly ready to repent, but their problem was that they could not remain repentant, that is, hold to that path of repentance. At their core, they did not grasp their sin, so their corrupt mind would inevitably lead them back to apostasy. The people would come back; how could Yhwh prevent them from leaving?

Only if they dedicated themselves to Yhwh's Torah could the people avoid straying. Yhwh used the words of the prophet and the judgment of death on the previous generations, for Israel and for the nations. As the people might have thought of death as a natural part of life, the prophets interpreted death as judgment from Yhwh. Death naturally forces the human being to examine what is important in life, and Yhwh argued through the prophets that service to Torah comes first. So Yhwh speaks to the prophet to continue to preach the judgments of Torah, in order that the people's way could be enlightened.

The prophets write on their hearts the words that put their tendencies to death. The word חצב, *xatsab*, usually means "hew," but in one instance it means "inscribe," as on stone (Job 19:24). Their mind was already on track for apostasy; a new thought pattern must be engraved in their brain.

V. 6 This key verse juxtaposes what Yhwh has requested since 4:1 with what the people thought they had been giving him. Yhwh only desired loyalty in meaningful actions, because they would profess adherence to Torah, not just fear of destruction. Kindness (חסד, *xesed*) and knowledge stand over and against sacrifice and burnt offerings because kindness implies generosity and selflessness, and knowledge implies dedication to a deep understanding of Yhwh and his teaching. Thus, these attributes display loyalty toward Yhwh.

In contrast, sacrifices try to manipulate the deity to win over his favor. They simply require fulfilling specific commandments, and do not necessarily imply loyalty after the sacrifices are made. One can see the correct mindset and loyalty toward Yhwh only through kindness manifesting knowledge of Torah.

V. 7 The untrustworthiness and disloyalty at the core of the people manifested itself in the first human, Adam. At no time in the biblical story did the human manifest true loyalty. Hence, Yhwh had no reason to trust that this generation would find themselves more loyal than any previous generation.

The phrase כאדם, *ke-'adam* can be interpreted multiple ways because of graphic similarities and word meaning.³ The initial letter -כ, *k-*, meaning "like," can easily be read by copyists as a -ב, *b-*, meaning "at." The word אדם, *'adam,* can be translated either as a proper name for the first human, "Adam," or as "a human." Thus, it can refer specifically to the rebellion of the first human in Gen 3 or generally to human rebelliousness. If we read this word as "human," the preposition is more likely to be read as "like." We end up with the following potential readings of the first part of this verse:

"*like* Adam, they transgressed the covenant"

"*at* Adam they transgressed the covenant"

"*like* a human, they transgressed the covenant"

I translate this as "like Adam" in order to highlight the continuity of sin; only one sin exists: rebellion. The Hebrew allows

---

³ Throughout the history of copying the Hebrew Bible by hand, copyists would often confuse certain pairs of Hebrew letters. When we translate, therefore, we must consider alternative meanings based on the other letter in the pair.

for ambiguity, so forcing a single English translation onto it does violence to the original text. Nevertheless, this meaning fits the context best. Human beings all transgress like the first human, which started in the first generation and continues to the present one. It did not happen once "in Adam," for which Hosea's audience only suffers the consequences. At the same time, the actions in Gen 3 offered a paradigm of human rebellion, that is, taking more than one needs, while ignoring Yhwh's provision and law. Hence, the hearers of this text must understand that they sin just as in Gen 3. Their life outside of "paradise" will not be returned to the garden by a quick profession of love and loyalty, but sin and exile will continue just as naturally and easily as it did at the fall of the first generation.

V. 8 The people's lack of loyalty toward Yhwh was manifested in their lack of charity and mercy toward their own people, whom they continued to fight and kill. The story of the bloodshed in Gilead reflected another example of bloodshed that led to fratricide. (See my comments on Hos 5.)

Fratricide and unjust slaughter were entirely too commonplace throughout Israel. When Jephthah of Gilead fought against Ammon in Judg 11, he crossed over the land of Ephraim, which, in Judg 12, angered the residents of the latter. Ephraim threatened that they would burn the houses of Jephthah with fire because he did not call on Ephraim to help in the Ammonite war (12:1). Jephthah of Gilead was angered by this reaction, in addition to the fact that Ephraim did not help in the fight against Ammon, and sent all the men of Gilead to fight against Ephraim (12:4). In the end, the Gileadites even killed the refugees of Ephraim who ventured into Gilead, simply because of their Ephraimite dialect. Ultimately, 42,000 Ephraimites were slaughtered (12:5-6).

Additionally, this verse obliquely refers to the story of Jacob and Esau, which further recalls brother-on-brother betrayal. This iniquity took over the people by their nature as children of Jacob. The rare root of the word "supplanted," עקב, *'QB*, comes from the same root as the name "Jacob." Just as Jacob "supplanted" the birthright from his brother (Gen 27:36), bloodshed took over whatever was good in Gilead. Since then, bloodshed, especially fratricide, took over ("supplanted") the people. Blood arose where Yhwh's people were supposed to be.[4]

V. 9 Hosea depicted the misconduct of the priests as murder, but the connection was not obvious at first. After so much allusion to the fratricidal wars from the past, depicting the priests as murderers lying in wait did not seem to follow. This chapter—even the whole Book of Hosea—tied the wickedness of the people to lack of knowledge of Torah, which Yhwh entrusted to the priests.[5]

The priests stood at the crux of the main problem: sacrifice and burnt offerings instead of kindness and knowledge of God (6:6). Like the other places mentioned in ch. 5 and in this chapter, Shechem also represented fratricide that came from twisted justice. In Gen 34, the namesake of this place, Shechem, violated Dinah, the daughter of Jacob. As a result, Dinah's brothers avenged her through trickery. They promised him to be allowed to marry Dinah, and his fellow citizens to become their brothers, if they submitted to circumcision. When they agreed to undergo the procedure and were healing, Jacob's sons slaughtered every male. While the son of Shechem committed a terrible crime, Jacob's sons overreacted to commit genocide. Moreover,

---

[4] See also Hos 1:4.
[5] See Hos 4:6-11.

Shechem's people had already become their brothers; hence, this genocide was, in fact, fratricide.

Shechem lay at the center of another episode of fratricide, in Judg 9. After Abimelech killed his brothers at Shechem, the people of Shechem made him king over them (9:5-6). Three years later, the Shechemites decided they no longer liked Abimelech as king, so they fought against him (9:23), and both Abimelech and the majority of the Shechemites ended up dead (9:53-57).

Lack of loyalty led to twisted justice and fratricide. The priests chose against mercy and kindness, and they did not teach these concepts to the people (ch. 4). The priests thus were, at best, accomplices to or, at worst, masterminds of the murder and fratricide that happened in the land. Their iniquity begat the iniquity of the people. Shechem, along with multiple other locations Hosea referred to, represented additional incidents of the same crimes.

V. 10 The Book of Hosea continued to make the case that rebellion against Yhwh's Torah was harlotry and the source of the sin found among the people. Moreover, this sin was not simply "disobedience" in an abstract sense, but manifested itself concretely as fratricide.

Rebellion resided inside Israel and Ephraim. More concretely, this recalled the clash at Gilead, referred to in v. 8, where Israel and Ephraim slaughtered each other. In a more general sense, this emphasized that the sin and rebellion found among all the people is harlotry—turning away from Yhwh.

V. 11 This looming judgment of Judah has not yet arrived in the narrative. One way to understand the abrupt remark about Judah's future is to read this as a later addition, after the original text of ch. 6 was written and after the defeat to Assyria had transpired. At the same time, the verse forces us to see Judah as another player in this drama. Judah was not spared because of their righteousness; Yhwh simply postponed their "harvest," or judgment. After the end of their captivity would be the time for Judah to prepare itself for judgment. At that point, Yhwh would decide on the paternity of Judah, based on the "fruit" produced at the time of reaping. Will the fruit of the field come from the plant Yhwh sowed, or from another sower who illicitly plowed his field? The judgement of the fruit would determine the fate of Judah.[6]

Judah could not be deceived by their current safety, relative to the pressure against the North. No part of Israel stood outside the rebellion and harlotry. The difference came because the time of harvest—judgment—had come to the North, but not yet to the South.

Ongoing rebellion

The people's sickness of rebellion and harlotry could not be cured. For a moment of repentance, it may go into "remission," but history shows that it would not disappear. Every generation has displayed the same symptoms.

Harlotry arose from disobedience and disregard of Torah. The priests were guilty as the perpetrators of ignorance that led to every crime. They bore the responsibility to teach the instruction that offered relief from lawlessness.

The Book of Judges is developing as a central source of evidence against the people over the course of this and the previous chapter. The narratives of fratricide between the Shechemites and the

---

[6] We already know that Babylon will attack Judah later in the story. Judah thus does not escape judgment.

followers of Abimelech (Judg 9), Gileadites and Ephraimites (Judg 11-12), and Israel and Benjamin (Judg 19-21), which enlarged the theme of mistreatment of the sons of Jacob and their new brothers, Shechem and his people (Gen 27), demonstrated how low the people can go. While Hosea declared judgment against the present generation of Israel, the case has been building for centuries. Given any moral outrage, the people were prepared to commit fratricide without any concern for justice or mercy beyond lip service.

Yet the people did not see the connection between the fratricide—both present and historical—and ignorance of Torah. They believed they fulfilled Torah when they performed sacrifices and burnt offerings, while ignoring kindness and knowledge of God. The latter two are related. Kindness comes from knowledge of God, which is Torah. Lack of kindness leads to human justice, and Hosea reminded us of the times when human justice quickly slipped into slaughter and genocide. Torah sets Yhwh's wise justice over corrupt human "justice."

Chapter 7

¹When I healed Israel, the iniquity of Ephraim and the evils of Samaria were revealed because they created a lie: a thief was coming, and a troop spread out outside.

²They do not mention to themselves that I remembered all their evil. Now all their deeds that were before my face have surrounded them.

³By their evil they please the king, and by their lies, the princes.

⁴All of them are adulterers, like an oven, burning from the baker. He stops raising its temperature, from kneading the dough until it is leavened.

⁵The day of our king, the princes made him sick by the heat from wine. He stretched out his hand with scorners.

⁶For they bring their heart close like the oven when they lie in wait. All the night their baker sleeps; in the morning it burns like a flame of fire.

⁷All of them will be heated like the oven and they will devour their judges, all of their kings have fallen, there is no one among them to call to me.

⁸Ephraim is mixing among the nations; Ephraim was a cake that was not turned.

⁹Strangers have eaten his strength, and he did not know; also, grey was sprinkled on him, and he did not know.

¹⁰And the beauty of Israel responded to his face, but they did not return to Yhwh their god, and they did not seek him in all this.

¹¹Ephraim was like a silly dove without sense; they called to Egypt and went to Assyria.

¹²As they go, I will spread my net over them; as they fly through the sky, I will bring them down. I will chastise as their congregation listens.

¹³Woe to them because they have fled from me; destruction is upon them because they sinned against me. Yet I will redeem them, though they have spoken lies against me.

¹⁴They did not call out to me in themselves when they were yelling on their beds; they gather together as foreigners¹ over grain and new wine. They turn away from me.

¹⁵And I chastened and strengthened their arms, so they consider evil against me.

¹⁶They will return, but not upwards. They were like a deceitful bow. Their princes will fall by the sword because of the wrath of their tongue. This is their derision in the land of Egypt.

Imagining disloyalty

Yhwh loved the people through guiding them with his teaching, even if they turned away from it. He proved his love by giving them all that they needed materially plus instruction for

---

¹ This verb can be translated two different ways. The Hebrew root גור, *GUR*, can mean "dwell as a foreigner" or "gather." In the Hitpael, this verb can mean "act like a foreigner" or "gather." That is, their religious gatherings and rites reveal a lack of loyalty to their "native" god, which betrays them as foreign.

sustaining a prosperous community. The people turned away, however, following others who they mistakenly believed sustained and taught them. So Yhwh had to bring them back to this initial teaching by forcing their hand, for which the people resented him.

Yhwh is the baker, and the people are his oven—his broken, useless oven. A baker needs a reliable oven, however, to make bread successfully. Normally, a baker does not show loyalty to this or that tool; he gets one that works and disposes of what does not. Yhwh, though, remained loyal to his "bad oven." He wanted to place the dough of his teaching in the people, and have it come out a lifegiving loaf. The rulers of his people, however, got overheated by lusting after those with power who would give them what they wanted. Yhwh hoped he could change the nature of the oven so it would not overheat so easily. While the people, especially its leaders, remained stubbornly disloyal, Yhwh battled this willfulness with his own irrational loyalty toward them.

The rulers of Israel got so excited about power and abundance, that they ruined any chance that a correct teaching could amount to something positive or even useful. A correct, wise teaching from Torah entered the oven of their minds but came out disgusting or even harmful. Yhwh could give them Torah and prosperity, and they would still think the work of their hands, whether foreign gods, pious priests, or brave kings, somehow brought these good things, because their ideas of strength and righteousness blind them to the truth.

Israel's deity would not desert them. He continued to chasten them to grant them an opportunity to come back. His instruction did not stop when they get out of line. When the people felt that Yhwh abandoned them because they were no longer safe, they misunderstand Yhwh. By pulling back on their prosperity and safety, he was teaching them that he alone provided both. Contrary to their beliefs, he was just as involved with them as before because he still imposed his teaching and judgment.

Commentary

V. 1 As Yhwh predicted, the profession of Israel's loyalty in 6:1 did not last. In that earlier passage they declared Yhwh's ability to heal them. As soon as Yhwh healed them and showed them mercy, however, they went out for gain, displaying their desire for illegitimate profit in this current verse. They did not trust in Yhwh's ability to provide for them. Their previous, apparent trust was proven to be a lie.

The verse depicts two ways in which they took for themselves. The "thief" represents their desire to steal from individuals. "Troop" expresses the desire to steal through war, when one steals from whole populations. No one was safe, as the people took from individuals and entire communities.

V. 2 They continued to lie to themselves by not admitting the disloyal nature of their deeds. They would not admit that Yhwh saw and remembered actions that they would like to hide even from themselves. Even though they ignored their misdeeds, the evil persisted, until finally the natural outcome took effect, and the people suffered. Hence the deprivation that they experienced resulted from their past actions, not malice on the part of Yhwh.

V. 3 Earthly rulers demand loyalty, so pleasing them renders any loyalty to Yhwh impossible. Such disloyalty to their god, because it contradicts Torah, is evil by definition. In ch. 1, the mother of the people acted in order to satisfy her lovers, the other gods. Here, the people do so to satisfy their king. Yhwh, as he stated, was fully aware of this disloyalty. The root cause is faith in kings and princes, which is incompatible with their god.

***

The baker and the malfunctioning oven (verses 4-10)

This section revolves around the image of a baker who works with a loaf and an oven that he heats with charcoal or wood. The baker must constantly monitor the heat of the oven and the leavening of the loaf. He is a master of timing. To bake the loaf, the oven must peak at a precise temperature at the same moment the loaf has finished rising. If the oven is too hot, the baker can bake the loaf immediately, burning it, or wait for it to cool, risking a foul-tasting, crumbly loaf as a result of letting it rise too long. For the expert baker, timing is everything, and he must be able to count on his oven.

The baker in this section represents Yhwh, and the oven, Israel, in whom Yhwh is trying to bake his loaf: Torah. As Torah-dough goes into the oven, the bread of good deeds—truth, kindness, and knowledge of God (4:1)—should come out. Instead, the oven gets too hot and he cannot bake it at all without ruining it.[2]

---

[2] A. A. Macintosh offers another reading, which interprets the baker as conspirators trying to overthrow the king. Certain courtiers conspired against the king to establish one that they wanted. They stoked the fires of the oven to prepare it for the revolution they were "cooking up." Moreover, they are the inattentive bakers who let the loaf rise too long. This fits in the context of the people's disloyalty because the conspirators mistakenly believe that they can take care of themselves and the government. Macintosh writes, "The fundamental mistake is the failure of such agitators to acknowledge that their behavior is adulterous (cf. v. 4); it is disloyalty to Yahweh, who alone could restore and heal the state" (A. A. Macintosh, *A Critical and Exegetical Commentary on Hosea* [Edinburgh: T & T Clark, 1997], 262-69).

Yhwh as the baker fits this metaphor better because the following verses do not refer to specific court intrigue, as Macintosh believes, with some good courtiers and some

V. 4 The people became overheated with lust, so no single husband could satisfy them. Any man with power, king or god, looked good to pursue for the sake of what he could give them. Overheated, they would ruin the loaf. In this instance, the baker finished feeding fuel to the oven so that its temperature could even out. In the meantime, he kneaded the dough, waiting for the loaf to rise before he placed it in the oven. But the oven is unreliable, because it overheats. It gets so hot that it will burn the loaf when the baker is ready to put it in the oven. Yhwh could not trust the people. In their overheated lust, they would not remain loyal; they would ruin what Yhwh wanted to create.

V. 5 The people found themselves in a dangerous position because of their rulers' desire for power. The king and princes used each other. The princes wined and dined the king to influence him, and the king reached out for assistance from his court, who would do his will for their own purposes, and would scorn him rather than respect him.

The wining and dining caused the "heat" in the oven in v. 4 that made the rulers burn with adultery and ruin the teaching of loyalty to the one god. One act of human injustice ended with genocidal fratricide when the leaders were overheated with righteous anger

---

bad, but to the consistent lack of loyalty of the people, beginning with the rulers. The main conflict throughout the book has been between the people, whom the rulers do not take care of, and Yhwh. Granted, following the leaders too faithfully will lead one away from Yhwh, but the entire people is under judgment. Macintosh implies that a subset of rulers has acted unfaithfully, rather than the entire people. Verse 4 states that "all of them," meaning all of Israel, are the adulterers who are the oven that is overheated. In addition, 7:1 responds to 6:1, as I mentioned above. The same problems that ch. 6 described, namely, lack of kindness and obedience to Torah among the people, stand at the center of this chapter. By following the instruction of the nations and other gods, the people neglected the instruction of Yhwh, and the rulers did not teach the correct instruction to the people (see 4:6-9).

and bloodlust.[3] The unjust way that the powerful exploited each other for their own gain caused the oven to be unreliable, ultimately ruining the baker's loaf. The mixed motives among the rulers led the people astray.

V. 6 The princes heated up their own hearts with adultery—overheating the oven. They were adulterers in the way that Hos 1-3 defined them: they looked for benefit from any potential source, without remaining loyal to the first and only source of their good things, Yhwh.

The baker builds up the fire at night so that the coals are just right by the morning, because if the oven is filled with flames, he cannot bake. Here Yhwh awoke to people enflaming themselves to adultery through mutual flattery, rather than a people ready to fulfill their role as the environment where Yhwh's work is manifested. Flaming fires made the oven unusable.

V. 7 The leaders' lust and mutual exploitation destroyed any viable leadership loyal to Torah. Because of the lack of loyalty to Yhwh, each one was looking out for himself, until no one was left. As the overheated, flaming oven, they devoured the judges and kings who were supposed to be kind, just, and knowledgeable. Torah did not emerge as what Yhwh wanted; instead, the oven burnt it to a cinder, destroying the leaders' ability to judge wisely or call out to Yhwh.

V. 8 Ephraim was incapable of following the will of Yhwh. They showed their adulterous nature by mixing with the nations, following any foreign teaching. As we read in ch. 1, the mother went to the gods of other nations for sustenance and comfort.

---

[3] See chs. 5-6.

Ephraim also showed this tendency as they went to the nations for the same.

Yhwh wanted a delicious loaf of actions that displayed loyalty to him. This uncooperative oven was ruining the whole process, requiring the baker to start over with a new loaf. If Ephraim was uncooperative, the actions Yhwh desires will not come out correctly.

Hence, they "baked" an inedible loaf. A good oven cooks evenly, while a bad one overcooks here and undercooks there. Yhwh tried to produce loyalty in them, but what came out was ruined, tainted by adultery. The cake is not Ephraim per se, but the actions of Ephraim that result from baking—or burning—the loaf of Torah that Yhwh put into them. The loaf did not burn because the baker neglected to turn it, but because the oven burned with lust as they went to mix with the nations, and so cooked the loaf unevenly and too quickly.

V. 9 Their loyalty, kindness, and knowledge of God were devoured by the other nations. Rather than provide for them, the foreign nations and gods consumed what Ephraim had. The people showed loyalty to foreign powers so that they would take care of them, and this display killed any loyalty they may have had toward Yhwh. Because of their deep sickness, they did not even know that loyalty to nations and to Yhwh together is impossible (cf. 2:7). The nations consumed their half-baked loyalty.

The "grey" on them was ash where they are burnt from overheating. They did not realize that their adultery, which "heated" the leaders' egos up and sent Ephraim after the nations instead of Yhwh, caused the loaf of loyalty to be ruined.

V. 10 In tragic irony, the people's best nature responded to Yhwh's teaching, but they did not seek him to carry out his will. Even though they gratefully accepted the dough, their broken nature could not produce anything resembling bread. They sought their own safety and security in mixing with the nations, the "strangers" of v. 9 who devoured their strength. Based on their past record, Israel would only seek their god again when their alternatives no longer appeared to be providing as well as they would like. They knew Yhwh would provide, but only turned to follow him when their other alternatives no longer produced what they desired.

* * *

V. 11 Ephraim exhibited their foolishness by flitting from one foreign protector to the next. The text moves from the metaphor of a useless oven to that of a foolish bird. From ch. 2, we saw that the sensible stance started with Yhwh as the source of all things. Otherwise, they flitted from one non-source of sustenance to another, from one nation to the next. Their nature matched the unpredictable flight of doves.

When the people followed their own will, they ended up enslaved. "Egypt" is an important theme, as it is mentioned twelve times between now and the end of the book. Furthermore, "Assyria" is paired with "Egypt" in five of them. On its own, Egypt represented multiple phases of Israel's past: the land of the people's enslavement, their redemption from Pharaoh, and their birth as Yhwh's people bound under Torah. Assyria was an even worse state. Despite the legacy of their fathers, the present generation would still "call to" a human king—even a latter-day Pharaoh—and ignore Torah. Assyria paralleled their ancient master to the

South, except that the people rejected Yhwh to submit voluntarily to the former.

V. 12 If the people wanted to remain in Yhwh's sphere, they would be acting with purpose. However, they flew all around like doves, trying to find whatever source of safety they could, and needed to be brought into control. Yhwh had to trap them to bring them back so they could hear the words of Torah again.[4] The trap should not surprise them; they heard the warning among the public chastisements of Torah.

V. 13 Though the people knew what Yhwh had in store for them, thanks to the public warnings from Torah in v. 12, they rebelled and sinned against him. They fled from him—the source of their sustenance and their punishment. Their nature compelled them to rebel.

Yhwh nevertheless sought to redeem them from the slavery they brought upon themselves. They called to Egypt and went to Assyria—who could not save them, but only could control and possess them—due to their inherent disobedience. In order to do so, they doubted the ability of Yhwh to provide for them, which constituted a lie against him. He resolved to take the people back as his own from these powerful nations, and so redeem them in spite of their lies.

V. 14 The people did not recognize Yhwh's sovereignty over the world, as they remembered Yhwh neither in bad times nor in good. When they were terrified, they did not call out to him, and when they celebrated the harvest, his name was not on their lips.

---

[4] Cf. ch. 3.

The Hebrew root "turn away from," סור, *SUR*, indicates more than snubbing; they apostatized against him. The Hebrew metaphor depicts a person on a path walking toward or away from their ruler, and so "turn" represents loyalty—if one turns *toward* a ruler—or rebellion—if one turns *away from* him. Thus, the Hebrew presents a profound rejection of Yhwh more than the English "turn away."

V. 15 Yhwh's instruction strengthened the people, though his teaching could be difficult. The Hebrew root here, יסר, *YSR*, includes the meanings "chasten" and "instruct"; therefore, Yhwh's actions were not simply punishment without teaching, and are not soft instruction. Their "arms" become strong because of this discipline. Their problems, their weaknesses, came from their inability to remain loyal to Yhwh, so any motivation to cleave to him gave them strength.

Yhwh naturally responded to rebelliousness with chastening, which the Hebrew links together in a way that English cannot. The root "chasten," יסר, *YSR*, sounds very similar to the root "turn away from" in the previous verse (v. 14), סור, *SUR*. Since the actions are connected by consonance, the link between the people's apostasy and Yhwh's instruction follows in the ear of the listener. Yhwh continued to teach and discipline them as his own children, for their own eventual good, even though they turned away from him.[5]

---

[5] If we choose to read against the Masoretic Text, we could read "I established" instead of "I chastened," assuming that a very minor, common spelling error entered the text during centuries of copying by scribes. The former comes from the Hebrew root יסד, *YSD*, and the latter, יסר, *YSR*, and the ד, "D" and ר, "R" are often confused by scribes because of their similar appearance. We would translate, then, "I established, I

In spite of the good result, the people resented Yhwh's means of teaching. While the people enjoyed this strength, they disapproved of Yhwh for employing such unpleasant means against them, such as invading nations. They considered him bad ("they consider evil against me"), ascribing malicious intent to his discipline. The correct student stays grateful to the teacher for the knowledge gained, not petulant because the experience was unpleasant.

V. 16 The people would go back to what they were, but this was not a good state. They naturally resided in a state of rebellion, disloyalty, and unreliability. By all appearances, they seemed to be a strong, reliable bow. When an arrow is shot from such a bow, though, no one knows where it will end up. It undermines the archer's actions, just as a bad oven will not bake reliably. Yhwh could not use Israel for his purposes because he could not hit the target he aims at.

The war that the people experienced came from the leaders' inability to rule on behalf of the people. To get what they wanted, the princes spoke the evil that they were thinking in the last verse, but in the end the people suffer because of the poor relations with neighboring peoples.

The people lived and acted, therefore, as slaves who never left Egypt. Hosea expressed the descent of their mind in geographical metaphors. In biblical geography, Egypt is always low, and Zion or Jerusalem is always high. Hence one goes "down" to Egypt and "up" to Jerusalem. While the people turned, they did not turn "up" toward the land of promise but "down" toward the land of slavery and death. They turned that direction because of the

---

strengthened their arms, yet they think evil against me," more forcefully underscoring Yhwh's development of the people and their ingratitude.

corruption in their hearts, which compelled them to seek slavery to their basic needs, rather than to desire freedom by focusing on Yhwh to provide these needs for them. They would go to any master who claimed to provide these needs—even if he would enslave them—rather than turn to their true lord who could provide all things for their livelihood and had no need of anything from them. They willingly chose this silly path, for which they were "derided."

Reliably unreliable

The people could only be counted on to act unreliably. When Yhwh taught them, they reacted consistently by doing the opposite. He could at least count on that mindset. A good oven acts predictably: such-and-such amount of wood will heat the oven to a certain temperature in a certain amount of time. Yhwh's oven heats inconsistently despite the same amount of wood placed in it. It may end up too hot or too cold, or change temperatures too quickly, ruining the bread. In the same way, a deceitful bow never sends the arrow to the same target. The rulers of Israel desired power so they could control resources; they became hot and cold quickly and unpredictably. A profession of love and loyalty in one moment completely disappeared in hours.

Yhwh, nevertheless, remained completely predictable. He met every action of disloyalty against his teaching with negative consequences. When they flew from one nation to another, a snare caught them. When the leaders burned with lust toward other earthly powers, the pain of war resulted. The very powers the rulers sought instead enslave and devour the people.

While Yhwh's teaching offers a way to life, greed eventually overcomes, enslaves, and destroys the greedy. Torah replaces the human being's desire to control and possess with the desire to trust and submit. Through trust and submission, one receives what one needs, but without losing one's soul, one's "teachability." Greed perpetuates more greed; the greedy never possess enough wealth, security, or power. Torah teaches and perpetuates the desire to learn and become better, submitting more and more to the teaching. Thus, Yhwh hopes Torah will fill the people with his spirit, replacing their current spirit of selfishness and greed.

Chapter 8

¹*The trumpet to your mouth, like the eagle on the House of Yhwh, because they have transgressed my covenant, and against my Torah they have rebelled.*

²*They will cry out to me, "My god! We, Israel, have known you!"*

³*Israel rejected the good; the enemy will pursue him.*

⁴*They made kings, but not from me; they made princes, but I did not know them. With their silver and their gold, they made idols for themselves, in order that they might be cut off.*

⁵*Your calf has rejected you, O Samaria. My anger has become hot against them. How long until they can be clean?*

⁶*For it is from Israel, a workman made it, so it is not God; for the calf of Samaria will become shards.*

⁷*For they sow the wind and they reap the whirlwind. It does not have any standing grain; the sprout will make no meal. If it produces, foreigners will swallow it.*

⁸*Israel is swallowed up, now they are among the nations like a vessel in which there is no delight.*

⁹*For they went up to Assyria, a lonely wild ass to it; Ephraim hired lovers.*

¹⁰*Even though they hired among the nations, now I will gather them. They were defiled a little from the burden of the king of princes.*

¹¹*Because Ephraim multiplied altars for offering sin-offerings, they were for him altars for sinning.*

¹²*I will write for him the great things of my Torah. They will be thought of as foreign.*

¹³*For the sacrifices of my gifts they sacrifice meat and they eat it. Yhwh did not desire them. Now he remembers their iniquity; he visits their sin. They are returning to Egypt.*

¹⁴*And Israel forgot his maker, so he built temples, and Judah multiplied fortified cities, so that I might send fire in his cities so it might devour their palaces.*

Powerless to help themselves

Humans want to hold on to power, believing that they deserve what they have, and that it belongs more appropriately to themselves rather than to others. As said in previous chapters, people spend their energy acquiring more power and keeping safe what they already possess.

Nevertheless, humans cannot prevent the anxiety that stems from recognizing their impotence in securing their power, and so look to other forces for help. Rather than letting go of their illusory power, they look for other ways to secure it, such as with idols and kings.

The will of Yhwh, over and against the people's power, remained central in this chapter. Loyalty depended on assent. As Yhwh commanded, so the people had to do. They tried to act like Yhwh, however, imposing their own will by choosing rulers to embody their will. Those human rulers did not carry out the will of the people, because they never had the power to do so. Not only did the people rebel, but they set up an alternative worse than what they had.

Once again, the people chose a king other than Yhwh, who enslaved them instead of granting them freedom to set up a system they hoped would benefit themselves. They put the power structure in place: kings, human laws, and idols. The leaders would work for themselves, however, not for those who established them. The so-called gods they set up will be entirely impotent and will let their devotees down, even while they demand offerings and rituals.

Rulers looked for gain from those inside and outside the nation. Thus, they exploited their citizens and angered their neighbors. Rebellion and civil war flourished inside the nation, and strife and invasion approached from outside. Those citizens who put their hope for prosperity in these overlords will be disappointed; worse, they will be exploited.

While this chapter functions for all of Israel, references to the Northern Kingdom predominate. In vv. 5-6 Samaria is in focus, and in v. 9 Ephraim specifically is accused of "hiring lovers" by turning to Assyria for defense. Moreover, Ephraim multiplied the "altars of sin" that manifest their deep ignorance of Torah. Yet, at the end of the chapter, both the Northern and Southern Kingdoms came into view, as they proved this problem is not isolated to the North but spread throughout the people.

Commentary

V. 1 The people rejected the instruction—Yhwh's Torah—that led to life. Therefore, the judgment of death was coming in the form of warfare. The trumpet symbolized the battle to which it called the people, and the metaphorical eagle on the House of Yhwh hungrily awaited the carrion resulting from the fight.

Yhwh did not need to send an invading army actively, as war is the natural outcome of not following Torah. As the people trusted in their leaders and military for defense, they became greedy and cocky, angering neighbors. They did not follow the instruction, the agreement they made with Yhwh, that would have kept them safe from disaster. By rejecting the one who would keep them safe, they subjected themselves to destruction.

V. 2 Israel would claim to know Yhwh, that he is their god. This is the same lip-service we saw in 6:1-2, where Israel declared their desire to turn back to their god. Their actions, in contrast, indicated that they have "known" another deity by following that god's teaching. Israel attempted to argue against Yhwh's claim in 4:1 that there is no knowledge of God in the land. The rest of this chapter built Yhwh's case against this claim of Israel's.

V. 3 The claim to have known Yhwh is incompatible with the fact that they turned away from him. At best, their claim to "know" this god is irrelevant in light of their actions. At worst, it is a blatant, wicked lie. Such a rejection made them vulnerable, and now the enemy chases them. The "pursuit" reminds us of 2:9, where Yhwh walled up his wife's way so she could pursue her "lovers" but not reach them. Now the enemy will pursue Israel—with no guarantee that they will not overtake Israel.

V. 4 The people set up according to their own will rulers who reflected the desires of the people. The kings and princes the people set up are beholden to the people's desires, enlarging the people's egos to run rampant. Today, congresspersons and MPs are beholden to the will of the people who elected them; their power completely depends on the support of their constituents.

As a result, they cannot challenge and teach the ones who put them into power. They are simply vessels of the people's so-called power.

Idols function the same way. They express the will of the people from a supposedly divine vantage point. Abraham Lincoln said about the Civil War, "In great contests each party claims to act in accordance with the will of God. Both *may* be, and one *must* be wrong."[1] Once people follow their own will and ascribe it to their god, they commit idolatry. In the example in the current verse, the people set up an idol in order to justify their own desires.

The people's will and ego flourished as a result, and hence separated them from Yhwh's will. They rejected Yhwh's teaching, which challenged and deflated their egos, which they preferred to follow instead of the teaching of their god.

The author played with Israel's claim to "know" Yhwh as they set up rulers, by countering that Yhwh never "knew" these rulers. While Israel's words rang hollow, Yhwh's "ignorance" of their rulers sounds foreboding. If these community heads worked according to Torah, they and Yhwh knew each other, but when they do not follow Torah, Yhwh had no knowledge of them.[2]

V. 5 The rulers of Samaria, the capital of the Northern Kingdom, set up a fetish that expressed their will, not Yhwh's. Yhwh commanded the people, and they rejected him. At the same time, the rebellious rulers led them to place their will upon the golden calf, but the impotent idol did not—could not—carry that will

---

[1] Abraham Lincoln, "Meditation on the Divine Will," as quoted in Joshua Wolf Schenk, *Lincoln's Melancholy* (New York: Houghton Mifflin, 2005), 198.

[2] See Gal 4:9, where Paul emphasizes "being known" by God rather than "knowing" God.

out. The idol effectively rejected the will of the people by doing nothing in the same way that the people rejected the will of Yhwh. Yhwh expressed his anger because both idol and people produced the same outcome: nothing.

In this context, "cleanness" takes on a nuanced meaning. The cleanness does not mean ritual cleanness as obedience to some sort of purity laws, but to obedience to the whole of Torah, of which ritual purity represents a part. Cleanness comes from wholehearted obedience, not legalistically following select rules.[3] Purity laws comprised a small portion of the will of Yhwh that the people had to carry out. To be clean, therefore, meant to put aside their own wills and egos in order to follow Yhwh's commandment to clean themselves as well as to perform obedient acts of חסד, *xesed*. It would likely be a long time (if ever) before they would be as clean as Torah demanded.

V. 6 This verse clarifies why the people would take so long to become clean. The two clauses show the motivation for the question raised in the last verse. They would take a long time to become clean, first, because their own workmen created a god for them, and second, because that god was impotent even to protect itself. As long as they insisted on the logic that they possessed the power to create a god with the power to protect them, they could not be obedient to anyone but themselves. They could not be clean and full of sin at the same time. Cleanness could only come after the painstaking transformation of this logic.

Compared to the infinite god, idols are a finite reflection of their finite creators. They are defined by a distinct beginning point,

---

[3] As Jesus said to the Pharisee in Gospel of Luke, "But woe unto you, Pharisees! for you tithe mint and rue and all manner of herbs, and pass over judgment and the love of God. These you ought to have done, and not leave the other undone" (Luke 11:42).

creation by a craftsman, and an end point, deterioration and destruction. They cannot bring any power that the people do not possess; a creation cannot hold more power than its creator. An idol cannot produce the virtuous fruit that the people should be producing.

V. 7 The work of those who follow their own ego ends in vanity.[4] Their efforts are motivated by vanity, so the results are vanity. They implant their transient, mortal egos into their creations, their idols, which hold no more power than their creators. They only concern themselves with survival, which inevitably fails. The idols that result cannot produce any outcome either. Just as mortal as their creators, they become "shards" (v. 6).

Only Yhwh created the grain and sprouts. The idols the people made could not provide food for them. Moreover, if Yhwh provided food, only he could keep them safe from invaders who would steal that food. The idol could neither produce nor defend.

V. 8 Because of their trust in a king and a god of their making, Israel remained defenseless. The nations captured them and took their goods. Thus, they were scattered among the other nations, empty of all the good things that Yhwh had provided them. Trusting in their own will and ego, rather than in the only one who could provide for and protect them, left them without protection from enemies. "A vessel in which there is no delight" is a purely functional, common vessel. Israel went among the nations, and there is nothing remarkable about them. Rather than carry the extraordinary blessing of their god in them as they bore

---

[4] The Hebrew word for vanity, הבל, *hevel*, also means "wisp of smoke; gust of air," which, though it does not appear in this verse, fits the context.

Torah, they looked like any other nation—as useful as any nation, but not for anything special.[5]

V. 9 Even beyond a king and a god of their making, the Northern Kingdom of Ephraim looked to the empire to the east as protection. Recalling ch. 2, this verse depicts the disloyalty of the people in terms of an unfaithful wife. Once she was no longer able to attract lovers in a straightforward way, she had to pay the lovers to come to her—a most unsuccessful prostitute! This reflects how Ephraim made deals with outside powers to protect them from invaders.

V. 10 The people's actions here in ch. 8 manifest the metaphorical marital disloyalty of ch. 3. Just as in ch. 3, Yhwh would act as a faithful husband; in spite of the blatant disloyalty of his wife, he would bring them back to himself. The defilement of the wife is another way she expressed her disloyalty. They turned to Assyria for protection (8:9) because of the kings and princes whom they selected without reference to Yhwh (8:4). In this way, their "small" defilement came directly from the "burden" of their kings and princes. Relative to the great defilement they caused by their lip-service to loyalty, their dedication to their kings was little. Nevertheless, Yhwh will remain loyal to her, in spite of her blatant rejection of him.

V. 11 They set up altars by their own will to expunge sin and guilt by their own hand. They multiplied altars just as they added rulers. As rulers were to keep them safe from enemies, altars preserved them from the wrath of the deity. Since they were not the ultimate judges or saviors, their altars' ability to relieve their guilt was nugatory. Yet in their minds, this action somehow

---

[5] Cf. the oven metaphor of ch. 7. As an ineffective oven, they could not produce an edible loaf. Here, they are a plain vessel that cannot bear anything special.

expunged their sin. So, either they set up idols for sin offerings out of ignorance of their own abilities, or they sought to dethrone Yhwh and make themselves their own judges. Neither excuse works, because Yhwh worked tirelessly from the beginning to educate them. Their ignorance was willed, further reflecting their deep sickness, which prevented them from getting well.

The redundancy of this verse is confusing, but the logic emphasizes the function of the altars with respect to Yhwh. The text repeats the phrase, מזבחות לחטא, *mizbaxôt lexaṭo'*, "altars for sin(ning)," playing on the double meaning of the second word.

The root חטא, *xaṭa'*, can either refer to "sin" or "sin offering," that is, the action that one commits and the necessary instrument for atoning for the action. We saw in ch. 4 how the author played on this double meaning. The priests benefitted from the sin offerings of the people, so they manipulated the people to multiply their sin. In the current verse, Ephraim multiplied altars for offering *sin offerings*, and as a result, they multiplied their *sin*.[6] When they set up their altars, they were for their idols, and therefore against Yhwh's will, as he just stated in v. 4.

V. 12 Yhwh could try to eliminate the people's ignorance with his instruction, but they could not hear him. The instruction of Yhwh, his Torah, sounded like a foreign language to them. The only solution to their sickness of ignorance was instruction, but

---

[6] The Qal of this verb with the sense "offer sin offering" is otherwise unattested. The Piel, however, is a transitive verb with this meaning. For example, Lev 6:19 (6:26 in English Bibles) uses the Piel participle with a direct object, "the one who offers it as a sin offering." For this reason, I am reading the verb in the current verse as an intransitive verb meaning "offer a sin offering."

their sickness made even comprehending the instruction impossible, let alone acting on it.

V. 13 They could not escape the loop of sin and sin offering, which enabled them to sin and benefit from it without consequence. Yhwh did not intend for a system where they sinned, sacrificed, and then enjoyed a good meal, but one where sin constituted a lapse in loyalty, which would be followed by contrite, obedient action. He did not want sin offerings.

Egypt, as mentioned above in 7:16, represented not only a geographical place but a system of slavery. In the former, it was a foreign place, just as the language of Yhwh's instruction sounded foreign to the people. They acted like they were enslaved Egyptians who could not understand Yhwh's Hebrew.

Moreover, Egypt only offered power without a savior. Pharaoh wielded all power and judgment but could not save. He killed, but did not give life; he enslaved, but did not offer freedom. When the Israelites separated themselves from Yhwh, they denied the source of life and freedom: Yhwh's teaching.

They enslaved themselves to the forces of the universe that they could not control, like Pharaoh, and that took away their will. Their kings and idols forced the people to serve them, while these powers acted capriciously, sometimes helping, sometimes oppressing. Neither could they free them from the powers of nature or the enemy to keep them safe. These powers took from their people without the ability to give.

V. 14 The farcical disconnect between the actions of Israel and the desires of Yhwh displayed the irony that the people tried to keep themselves safe while ignoring the one who offered safety. Israel wished to express itself by building and creating, yet they forget that Yhwh created them. Ironically, their desire to build temples—even for Yhwh—expressed a rejection of Yhwh's will, just like their desire to build altars for sin offerings in v. 11. They wanted to own and surround the place where Yhwh resided, which added to their own power. When the deity's location was controlled by those in power, the weak could access it without going through these elite people. They were literally the gatekeepers for their god. This chapter defined idols, altars, and now temples as malignant outgrowths of the people's ego.

Their understanding dragged them far from the truth. The Hebrew verb here ויבן, *wayyiven*, bears a double meaning, either "so he built" or "and he understood." Not only did they build temples, therefore, but the logic of temples took over their thoughts, pushing Yhwh out. Building temples resulted from their corrupt understanding.

Moreover, they built fortified cities to protect themselves rather than count on Yhwh for help. These fortifications only kept the people relatively safe; enemies could overwhelm such defenses at any time, with Yhwh's help.

The combination of Israel plus Judah, and the parallel of "temples" and "fortified cities," expressed how rampant the problem was, and how complete the judgment would be. The disloyal desire to preserve oneself extended from the Northern Kingdom, Israel, where they built temples, to the Southern Kingdom, Judah, where they built fortified cities. Moreover, temples counted on the cities in which they were built for protection. Hence, the whole people was infected with this disloyalty, manifested in its desire to control their god and keep themselves safe, as opposed to submitting to Yhwh and letting him save them.

Yhwh threatened to make his point quite forcefully, as he could easily destroy the cities by sending fire inside of them. While the people might pray to the god inside the temple, that god would not save them, and the cities would not protect them when the attack came from inside. He displayed the people's ignorance when they tried to determine their own safety.

Other paths lead nowhere

The people developed a complete and elaborate religious and political system that produced nothing good. The people chose the leaders as extensions of their egos, to make themselves safe, and then those leaders set up temples and religious rituals to keep themselves safe and secure at the expense of the people. They additionally fortified themselves against attacks from enemies. The people intended for the stream of power and wealth to pool within themselves, and the leaders of the people reaped the benefits. Nevertheless, they could not keep themselves fed or safe from enemies.

While they submitted to Yhwh in their words, their actions displayed loyalty to another god. Their adherence to some of Yhwh's Torah misled them into thinking that Yhwh clearly saw their loyalty. On the contrary, the fact that they did not adhere to most of his Torah showed disloyalty. Yhwh had to teach them that obedience in cleanliness rituals alone did not imply that they were "clean." Their adulterous nature sullied them: they would rather depend on foreign kings than on Yhwh.

Yhwh will remain loyal, but that could only help so much when the people insisted on turning their backs on him. Their mistaken belief that they were following Torah rendered them unteachable, and, as a result, Yhwh could not heal them.

The author reminded listeners of their impotence through the metaphorical geography of Egypt. The power of death over the Israelites that Egypt held represented the power the Israelites desired. To wield this power themselves, they set up their own system of government and religion that should have protected them, but contradicted Torah. As a result, they were doomed to be taken captive to Assyria, their new Egypt. They did not learn that Torah could only be received once they left Egypt and the power Pharaoh represented. By forming themselves into a semblance of Egypt, they made themselves like Egyptians, foreigners unable to grasp even the words of Torah.

Chapter 9

¹Do not be happy, O Israel, for joy like the other peoples, for you have whored away from your god; you have loved payment on every threshing floor of grain.

²Threshing floor and winepress will not take care of them,¹ and new wine will fail in it.

³They will not dwell in the land of Yhwh, but Ephraim will return to Egypt, and they will eat what is unclean in Assyria.

⁴Let them not pour out wine offerings to Yhwh, and let them not pass their sacrifices to him; they are like the bread of mourners for them. All his food defiles. Because their bread is for their appetite, it will not enter the house of Yhwh.

⁵What will you do in the day of meeting or in the day of the festival of Yhwh?

⁶For behold, they went because of destruction. Egypt will gather them; Memphis will bury them. The nice thing of their silver, nettles will possess them, thorns in their tents.

⁷The days of visitation have come; the days of recompense have come. Israel knows. The prophet is a fool—the man of the spirit, crazy—over the greatness of your iniquity and the greatness of animosity.

⁸The watchman of Ephraim was with my god; the prophet is the trap of the fowler on all his ways, animosity in the house of his god.

---

¹ Lit. "will not shepherd them."

⁹*They have deeply corrupted themselves, like the days of Gibeah. He remembers their iniquity; he visits their sin.*

¹⁰*Like grapes in the wilderness I found Israel; like the first fruit in the fig tree in her beginning I saw your fathers. They came to Baal-Peor and they were separated for shame. They were detestable things when they loved.²*

¹¹*Ephraim—their glory flies around like a bird, from birth, from the womb, from conception.*

¹²*Even though they raise their children, I will bereave them of people; for indeed woe to them when I turn³ from them.*

¹³*Ephraim, just as I saw for Tyre, is planted in a pleasant pasture, but Ephraim is to bring out his children to a murderer.*

¹⁴*Give to them, O Yhwh, what you will give. Give to them a bereaving womb and dried-up breasts.*

¹⁵*All their evil is in Gilgal, for I hated them there; over the evil of their deeds from my house I will drive them out; I will not continue to love them, all their rebellious princes.*

¹⁶*Ephraim is struck. Their root is dried up that it cannot produce fruit. Even when they give birth, I will kill the beloved ones of their womb.*

---

² I am reading באהבם, *ke'ohovam* as the preposition *ke-* followed by an infinitive construct with a subjective third-person plural pronominal suffix, "their." This preposition in this context can mean "when."

³ I am reading this סור for שׁור, which are pronounced identically in Hebrew, *sûr*.

¹⁷My god will refuse them because they did not listen to him, so they will be wanderers among the nations.

The illusion of idolatry

Did the people really have so much power that they could turn nature itself against them? Wouldn't it have been more natural to assume the tide of nature would ebb and flow no matter what this impotent people might do?

Torah, Yhwh's instruction, should have taught them the wisdom that grasps the reality of nature. Namely, this teaching should have brought the truth about actions and consequences into clear focus: when you hoard good things to preserve yourself, others go without until they no longer have enough to survive. When others might want to hoard the same things, you make rivals of them, until they become your enemies seeking to destroy you. When you dedicate your unjust gain to other deities as means of gaining even more, you definitively show that you lack the sense or wisdom that Torah tries to teach. This incorrect placement of loyalty defines idolatry.

If the people had submitted to their own impotence, things would have gone well; the problem arose when they fell into precisely what Torah warned against. The first to believe that they could control nature were the powerful. They began to divert resources from the weak to supplement what they had, and so controlled their future. They dedicated some of those resources to their chosen gods, the Baals, for sacrifice. The good foods for sacrifices were turned over to the priests and filled the tables of their piety-riddled banquets. In the meantime, the poor suffered. Starvation and deprivation resulted. Others rose in power and tried to take what the rich had, causing war. The next generation could not survive.

The solution was for the strong to give to the weak, and for the weak to pass along to the weaker. If they served Yhwh, the pious feast would have been offered to the poor, rather than to fellow-elites. Neighbor would have shared with neighbor in times of deprivation, and so they could experience fellowship instead of rivalry. Generosity would have established alliances with others and brought prosperity to all.

The myth of a life-giving Baal overpowered the people's wisdom, and Yhwh would counteract it strongly in the next generation. Verses 11-16 directly targeted the death of the next generation. Their god would target the womb, the breast, and the children themselves to make his point that life could not come from their works. The seeming cruelty of these verses only appears when we forget that the people decided to let go of those things that give life. Yhwh was not taking aim at their children; the people rejected those things that gave their children life, without a thought for their own children's needs. Like a generation who loves living large and then passes the environmental and financial debt on to the next generation, these parents' actions led to the natural consequences for their sons and daughters.

Commentary

V. 1 Following Baal may or may not be a good thing, depending on who one's father is. For a Canaanite, remaining loyal to the god of his nation could testify to his virtue; an Israelite devoting himself to Baal revealed deep betrayal. Once Yhwh delivered the children of Israel from slavery and made them a people, they owed their existence to him, and when he taught them how he provided food and clothing to them, they were obliged to him out of gratitude. They turned and praised Baal, however, as we saw in ch. 2.

Thus, the sons of Israel could not rejoice at the bounty like the Canaanites because their rejoicing came at the expense of their loyalty to Yhwh; they whored. The Canaanites remained loyal because they stuck to the teaching they received, that Baal provided their bounty, and so praised him out of ignorance of Yhwh's Torah. The Israelites praised Baal in spite of knowledge of Torah, which they deprived themselves of (4:6), and which taught them that Yhwh provided all things. Hence the same action manifested the loyalty of the Canaanites and betrayed the deep sickness of Israelites. Any god could buy the latter's loyalty with a bit of food. The rejection of Torah doomed them.

V. 2 When the bounty of food and drink excited the people, they were missing the most important gift from Yhwh: his Torah. This verse described what would not take care of them: "threshing floor," representing food, and "winepress" and "new wine." While other peoples rejoiced in receiving this provision from their fickle gods, Yhwh did not want his people to remain simple. Food and drink would appear and disappear in alternate bountiful and lean times. If they depended on Torah, they could count on having enough. Furthermore, this teaching endlessly provided instruction and guidance in the correct path. Hence, Torah shepherded them and did not fail.

V. 3 Rejecting Torah resulted in living without the teaching that saved them and offered wisdom. Torah explained that when Israel transgressed it, they could no longer live in the land. By rejoicing over the food and drink they provided with their own hands, they turned their backs on Yhwh, the one who kept them safe.

Their enemies, the Assyrians, would take them captive, and the Israelites would not be able to follow Torah, even if they wanted to. As mentioned in 8:5, above, purity laws only represented one small part of the demands of Torah. This fact notwithstanding, Assyria would make it impossible to follow even this small part of Yhwh's instruction. The people would enter a metaphorical Egypt with only the instruction of a human king to follow.

Egypt represented Israel's primordial slavery. They did not exist as Israel until Yhwh brought them into existence and offered them his Torah.[4] The verse seems to contradict itself, that Ephraim will return to *Egypt* and eat unclean things in *Assyria*. Israel cannot be in two places at once, but in either country they would exist in the same state: separated from Yhwh, subjugated as a people to a human king. When they rejected Torah, they removed themselves from their relationship with Yhwh by serving a human ruler.

V. 4 Sacrificing to Yhwh, in the context of the rejoicing over the winepress and threshing floor, displayed no virtue, but further ignorance of Torah. While the people believed that the bounty they received deserved a celebration, Yhwh was ready to mourn because of the betrayal that that rejoicing represented.

When they believed the food came from Baal's bounty, or any source other than their god, the food defiled them. They thought that the food came to them because they deserved to have their bellies full, and not because of the gift of Yhwh. Defilement implied an unclean state, and thus prevented them from entering the temple. Their disobedience and betrayal of Torah made the people—not just the food—unclean.

V. 5 The people had nothing to present to Yhwh. They had no proper sacrifice because they rejected him, and this attitude sullied their offering in turn. They knew how to celebrate the bounty of food and wine with Baal but did not know how to commemorate

---

[4] Geography functions metaphorically, as explained in 7:16 and 8:13.

Yhwh's gift of Torah to them. If they even showed up to Yhwh's festivals, their hands would be empty of what was most important: loyal deeds.

V. 6 We see again those actions that resulted from rejecting Torah: defeat by enemies and the end of their bounty. Their enemies would destroy them, and they would revert to their "Egyptian" state, even dying there as Memphis "buried" them. Not only would they die, but their property and dwellings would be abandoned; no generation would exist to possess them. Their lineage would die along with them, as nature overcame their abandoned settlements.

V. 7 The prophet related Yhwh's judgment to the people as Yhwh's spirit spoke through him, but the people's ignorance prevented them from hearing him. The prophet announced Yhwh's "visitation," when he would come with his judgment. Israel was informed of what would come. As they rejected Torah, though, they neither heard the judgment nor understood it. Their minds had become corrupt. The word of the prophet sounded like nonsense, crazy-talk. "Iniquity" and "animosity" pointed again to their betrayal of Torah.

V. 8 As much as the people thought the prophet was a "fool" (v. 7), he spoke on God's behalf—whether good news or bad. As the "watchman," he warned the people when danger was coming.[5] Indeed, danger was coming. Since the people were flying around like dumb birds (7:11), the prophet was the one who trapped the bird and sealed its fate. In vv. 4-5, the animosity of the people was linked to their iniquity; here, the animosity was located in the temple. Hence, their rebellion caused animosity.

---

[5] Cf. Ezek 33.

The prophet underscored the agency of Yhwh in the people's woes, warning them that their misfortune came because they demonstrated that another god was their father. The watchman was with "my" god, that is, the god of the narrator. The prophet brought the truth of the people to them in the temple. He condemned their ways in the temple of "his" god, and so undermined any notion that Ephraim remained faithful to the prophet's god. He trapped them in their ways in the place where they were performing these selfish, rebellious actions. The words of the prophet judged the people who thought they were serving their father, Yhwh, when they were, in fact, sons of a different god.

V. 9 Their rebellion resulted in self-serving violence. "The days of Gibeah" referred to the fratricidal war in Judg 19-21, when a horrible crime led not to justice but exploded into genocide.[6] Ignoring Yhwh's actions and fighting against his inevitable judgment led to extreme violence, in the narrator's past and present. Even though the present chapter "only" described the people looking for help among the nations, bloodlust, not justice, lay at the base of their desire. Based on the habits of the people, the resulting war would not produce justice but genocide. Ephraim would see the fruits of their unjust self-righteousness.

V. 10 The people showed their corruption from very early on. Yhwh "found" Israel when he brought them out of Egypt into the מדבר, *midbar*, "wilderness," where they spent 40 years. Israel—depicted here as a woman—was new and budding. In the last year of their sojourn, unfortunately, they turned to Baal at Baal-Peor.[7] They looked to another deity to provide for them. This disloyalty made them unclean, and their love was only love so-called; their

---

[6] I discussed this episode at length in my comments on Hos 5.
[7] Num 25.

loyalty ruined the idea of actual loyalty. Like in v. 8, their so-called acts of love and devotion only implied loyalty to a father other than Yhwh. Their love, because of its falsehood, was detestable to Yhwh.

V. 11 Ephraim was fated for corruption. Not only were they corrupt from birth, but it was established even earlier. Their glory was, in fact, not glory. The Hebrew plays on the verbal link between כבוד, *kavôd*, "glory," and כבד, *kaved*, "heavy," as it contrasted Ephraim's glory with a bird. The "weightiness" of "glory" cannot flit around with the lightness of a bird. The bird, as it hops from one perch to the next, further represented the people's inability to stay with one master, one god (9:8 and 7:11). They could not gain glory by moving from one prestigious master to another; to the contrary, moving from one god to another proved that they had no weight, no glory.

This trait was rooted in Ephraim's deepest being. The writer moved backwards in time, from the day of birth, to the period of gestation, to the day of conception, proving literally that the corruption belonged to the core of the people.[8] Even when Yhwh "found" the people in the מדבר, *midbar*, "wilderness" (v. 10), the seed of corruption already dwelt in them.

V. 12 The people would like to control the next generation, the future of their people, but they would learn that it was beyond their power to do so. Yhwh would deprive them of their children, as their inability to control their future devastated them. Life would no longer reside with them without Yhwh, the one who

---

[8] We find a similar technique in Job 3:3, where Job cursed not only his birth, but the night of his conception. This reverse-chronology emphasizes the person's entire existence by backing up before one's birth. Just as one can curse a people by cursing their forefather, we can curse someone's existence by cursing their conception.

gave life to the next generation. This death did not come as punishment per se, but as a natural demonstration of the people's lack of power compared to Yhwh. When they turned from Yhwh, he effectively turned from them.

The next generation would be bereft of people, just as half a generation disappeared at the hand of Cain. The author exploited the double meaning of אדם, *'adam*, since it can mean "human" or "Adam," so that we can read this verse as either "deprive them *of humans*" or "deprive them *more than Adam*."[9] The first interpretation means that the next generation would not have people; the nation would stand on the brink of extinction. The second implies that the devastation of Adam personally, as he lost his son at the hand of another son, would be reflected in the current generation of humans. Their powerlessness would be felt acutely as their nation would lose a generation and their individuals lose their sons.

V. 13 Ephraim was not a victim of circumstances or of an angry god, but the author of their own destruction by their unwillingness to submit. Tyre was set in a comfortable, safe location, close enough to land to survive, but far enough away to remain secure from invasion. Ephraim, too, sat in an area where they could live and prosper. Their circumstances provided security, if they only accepted them. They chose, though, to turn themselves over to the forces of nature, Baal, who could not provide for them. As a result, their children were dying; by their actions, they effectively handed their children over to murderers.

V. 14 As they lauded their demanding gods and oppressive rulers, they deprived themselves and each other of the good things of the

---

[9] Cf. 6:7.

land. Thus, their children were not necessarily killed outright, but died the long death of starvation. Their mothers could provide for their babies neither in the womb nor after birth, so their children were stillborn or starved as they lacked food and security. The next generation would disappear as the people separated themselves from Yhwh, the giver of life. All that they would get would come from Yhwh.

V. 15 Yhwh would deprive them of his love and protection because their leaders betrayed him. They manifested their disloyalty through their cult from the beginning. Gilgal represented one of the pre-temple worship sites where, for example, Samuel used to offer worship.[10] For Yhwh, though, these places had a bad reputation, as we saw above in 4:15. The people believed they were worshiping Yhwh, but they worshiped other gods in fact because they were looking only for their own security and gain. From Gilgal to the temple of Hosea's time ("my house"), the people displayed the same disloyal behavior. Their god sent them out, no longer loving them. He focused his wrath on the rulers because they disrupted the system by looking out exclusively for their own good.[11]

V. 16 The actions of the people set their fate in motion. The sickness sat deep at the root, so that the next generation, the "fruit," would not come. Even if it were to come, the children would die, like in v. 14. The prophet thus tied the consequences already laid out in vv. 11-12 to the cultic offenses and the manifestation of their disloyalty here. As they worshiped other gods who could not give life, they themselves would not be able to see another generation.

---

[10] 1 Sam 7:16.

[11] See ch. 4.

V. 17 The people lost their tie to the source of life when they refused to submit to the teaching of Yhwh. This verse states that the god of the prophet would refuse them because they lived for themselves and for control of their future. Even though they entreated for selfish reasons their deity to protect them from harm, they would lose their home to nature and to enemies, from which those so-called gods could not save them. They would live like the birds they already resembled, flying from one place to the other, homeless.

The next generation in jeopardy

Disobedience to Yhwh resulted in the eventual annihilation of the people. One does not need to imagine the consequences as a direct intervention of the deity, but by Occam's razor we see that the people's misfortune came from looking to control their own destiny rather than seeing the wisdom of submitting to reality.

The chapter tied birth and life to death and mourning, as Yhwh gave life to the first generation, but would allow the next generation to die out. We hear how Yhwh first "found" Israel as grapes in the מדבר, *midbar*, "wilderness," but they just as soon turned away from him to Baal (v. 10). At several points (vv. 12-14, 16), Yhwh expressed the people's fate as the preemptive destruction of the next generation. The people rebelled against Yhwh's Torah now, and the next generation would not exist. Extinction would result from their acts of disobedience.

The people's end was manifested by becoming an un-people, reversing their "birth" at the Exodus. The theme of captivity occurred multiple times in this chapter (vv. 3, 6, 11), significantly, before the references of destruction for the next generation. The image of Egypt as the symbol of their non-existence as a people (vv. 2, 6), and the birth that came after Egypt (v. 10), together expressed how the people were made and how they could be unmade. When they would go into captivity, they would enter another Egypt, where their captors would impress their own law upon them, and the people would no longer be able to show loyalty to Yhwh via obedience to Torah. The next generation would disappear because resources were depleted by their parents' hoarding, and so the people would be unmade when captured.

Chapter 10

¹*Israel is a barren vine; he bestows fruit on them. According to the multitude of his fruit, he multiplied altars. According to the goodness of his land, they made standing stones good.*

²*Their heart is divided; now they will be ashamed. He will bring down their altars. He will destroy their standing stones.*

³*For now they say, "We have no king because we did not fear Yhwh. And the king, what will he do for us?"*

⁴*They spoke words, empty oaths, cutting a covenant; so judgment sprouts up like poison over the furrows of my fields.*

⁵*For the calves of Beth-Aven the dwellers of Samaria will sojourn, because its people mourned over it, but its priests will rejoice over it, over its glory when they go into exile from it.*

⁶*Even it shall be taken to Assyria, a sacrifice to the king who contends; Ephraim will take on shame, and Israel will be ashamed of his advice.*

⁷*Samaria: her king is cut off, like stubble on the face of the water.*

⁸*And the high places of Aven[1] are destroyed, the sin of Israel. Thorn and thistle will grow up over their altars. And they will say to the mountains, "Cover us!" and to the hills, "Fall on us!"*

---

[1] This can also mean "wickedness," hence the phrase can mean "high places of wickedness."

⁹*From the days of Gibeah you have sinned, O Israel; there they stood, that the war against the sons of iniquity² might not overtake them in Gibeah.*

¹⁰*In my desire I will chastise them; peoples will be gathered against them, when they will be bound to their two iniquities.*

¹¹*Ephraim is a trained calf who loves³ to thresh, and I passed over the goodness of her neck. I will ride Ephraim, Judah will plow, Jacob will break the clods for it.*

¹²*Sow⁴ for yourselves to righteousness, reap for a mouth of loving-kindness. Break up the fallow ground for yourselves for it is time to seek Yhwh until he comes to cast righteousness for you.*

¹³*You plowed wickedness, iniquity you have reaped, you ate the fruit of lies because you trusted in your way and in the multitude of your warriors.⁵*

¹⁴*A tumult will arise among your people, and all your fortifications will be destroyed, like Shalman's destruction of*

---

² I read here with most scholars who read עלוה, *'LWH*, as עולה, *'WLH*, with the two middle consonants transposed.

³ This verb is a feminine singular participle. Its form is peculiar because of the final י "yod." Without the vowels, the easiest way to interpret this verb would be "I loved," but it does not fit easily in the context. See notes on this verse, below.

⁴ This verb—as well as the following verbs in this verse—is in the second-person, masculine plural.

⁵ The first three verbs ("plowed," "reaped," and "ate") all appear in the plural of the second person, while the final verb and possessives ("trusted," "your way," and "your warriors") appear in the masculine singular of the second person.

*Beth-Arabel on the day of war—a mother was dashed to pieces against her children.*⁶

¹⁵*Thus Beth-El did to you because of the wickedness of your wickedness, and in the morning the King of Israel was utterly cut off.*⁷

Yhwh judged their empty promises

The people's actions once again underscored their lip service; saying the right things, they acted as wicked as ever. In 6:1-3 they proclaimed Yhwh's goodness and power, yet they returned quickly to perform sacrifice rather than acts of kindness. They cried out to their god in 8:2 that they have "known" him, even though Yhwh asserted in 4:1 that there was no knowledge of God in the land. Now they regurgitated imprecations against their king—but only after Yhwh proved him to be incapable of saving them. Their lack of correct action by itself brought them under judgment, but their correct words demonstrated they should know better.

Verse 2 states the thesis for this section: the people's disloyalty caused their destruction. The preceding verse lays out the current state, namely, while Yhwh provided everything, the people followed other gods. The rest of the chapter offers data to support Yhwh's claim. They testified against themselves by admitting they trusted a useless king over Yhwh. Their empty promises were judged, and those who made these promises empty—first and foremost, the king—would be carried into exile to Assyria. This activity of fighting an ill-conceived and disobedient war followed

---

⁶ Both second-person references ("your people" and "your fortifications") are in the masculine singular.

⁷ The second-person references here ("to you" and "your wickedness") are both in the plural.

a pattern since the war against the Benjaminites at Gibeah. When Yhwh directed them, and they worked according to his will, they prospered; in contrast, they suffered when they worked according to their own hearts.

The prophet accused the people of idolatry, of worshiping golden calves at altars. While Moses took too long to come down from the mountain with Yhwh's Torah in Exod 32, the people got impatient, and so took matters into their own hands and immediately put a god in place (Exod 32:1). The people clearly worshiped idols, images—yet Aaron declared that these brought them out of Egypt, and he dedicated a feast of Yhwh to them (32:4-5). In their minds and words, they were worshiping Yhwh, but according to Yhwh, it was idolatry and worshiping false gods. Simply calling a god "Yhwh" did not legitimize worship. They wanted to worship their "dependable" god on their own timeline rather than wait for Moses and Torah. In their minds they were faithful, but their choice of worshiping now rather than waiting for Yhwh and following Torah displayed a lack of trust and obedience.

The text of 1 Sam 8, which narrated Israel's first desire for a king, functions as a backdrop for grasping Hos 10. Yhwh granted the people a king in spite of, or even because of, their rejection of him. Furthermore, that chapter linked the desire for a king not only to disobedience of Yhwh, but also to idolatry as they "served other gods."[8] This chapter takes for granted the link between loyalty to a king and to another god.

Yhwh argued that the people's actions showed fealty to the respective god, not the profession of their mouths, because a god

---

[8] 1 Sam 8:8.

represents a teaching. Baal-worship demanded standing stones and regular sacrifices, but not taking care of the poor; Yhwh demanded taking care of the poor, but not standing stones. If someone worshiped standing stones or neglected the poor, if the person claimed loyalty to Yhwh and indeed called his god "Yhwh," his actions worshiped Baal because they followed that god's teachings. The golden calves at Sinai were Baal because Yhwh is not represented by golden statues, even though they called the calves "Yhwh," but by his Torah, which they rejected in their impatience.

Changing the polytheistic paradigm

The scenario in Hos 10 built on the typical polytheistic story while simultaneously undermining it. In the typical story, the army backed by the stronger god(s) wins.[9] Hence a battle between two armies came down to the stronger of two deities (and whatever coalitions they could build). The earthly battle manifested the heavenly counterpart.

Yhwh claimed agency in everything that befell Israel, however, win or loss. This aimed at the fundamental misunderstanding of the people. While the bad things that happened may have appeared to come at the hand of an enemy nation, a natural disaster, or a foreign god, Yhwh caused them. As we saw in ch. 2, they thought that Baal caused one thing, while Yhwh caused another. When one deity was stronger, that deity's will would be done. Hence the Israelites hedged their bets and worshiped both. In fact, only Yhwh acted, and the other gods and nations were subject to him. They acted according to his will. When the land

---

[9] We see this play out in *The Iliad* in the quarrel between the gods, for example, in the feud between Athena and Apollo, protectors of the Achaeans and the Trojans, respectively.

prospered, Yhwh caused it; when the Assyrians attacked, as we see in this chapter, Yhwh caused it.

On the one hand, the people thought that they could see clearly—based on this paradigm—that the god of Assyria defeated the god of Israel. The enemy soldiers captured the golden calves of Samaria, brought them home to Mesopotamia, and sacrificed them to their god.[10] While the people mourned, they understood how the world worked and why things turned out the way they did.

On the other hand, Yhwh undermined this paradigm by teaching Israel that they did not worship him in their cult. He was the god of Sinai and Torah; worshiping him meant following his teaching by their actions of loyalty and חסד, *xesed,* "kindness." Their actions followed a different teaching; therefore, they could not be worshipping him.

Thus, the Assyrian god beat the Israelite god. *The functional Israelite god, though, was not Yhwh.* It was a weak god constructed with their hands: a golden calf, not the author of Torah. Yhwh stood above both, orchestrating the defeat of the Israelite idol at the hands of the Assyrian army.

Commentary

V. 1 The people's acts of piety revealed the desire to manipulate, not faithfulness. When Yhwh granted them bounty to enjoy, they built cultic sites. The cult represented a desire to show their faithfulness, even though the criteria for correct action, since 4:1, has been truth, kindness, and knowledge of God. Using the

---

[10] It is not a coincidence that the Israelites worshiped golden calves at Sinai and in Samaria. The former episode provided the basis for the critique by subsequent prophets against the latter.

bounty for the sake of the needy is conspicuously missing. Rather than share and provide for others, they built up their religious façade. They could not be following Yhwh's Torah.

Focus on cult rather than on fulfillment of Yhwh's teaching reflected their self-righteousness. The people began with nothing, unable to produce anything, yet Yhwh made fruit come forth. As the fruit increased, however, the more the people acted inappropriately and increased their idolatry. When Yhwh allowed the land to produce, the people multiplied the holy places for their gods. They kept the produce for themselves, but in such a way that they could tell themselves that they used it for their god, and so followed the teaching of their god(s)—not that of Yhwh.

V. 2 Yhwh would bring down their so-called holy places; he would not protect what was not his. They did not erect standing stones out of obedience to Yhwh; he never commanded them to do so. Logically, then, they erected stones out of loyalty to some other teaching, that is, another god. Their swiftly-changing loyalty for their various gods would make them ashamed when they confront their unique god, Yhwh, just as their mother, the land, was ashamed. Furthermore, the looming attack by the Assyrians would reveal the worthlessness of their worship to impotent gods. Yhwh took ownership of the destruction of these holy places. As Yhwh already explained in 5:14, they were destroyed *not* because of Yhwh's *inability* to protect them, but because of his *ability* to annihilate them. Their destruction showed Yhwh's strength, not his weakness.

V. 3 Words renouncing the king seemed to get the people back on the right track. Instead of trusting Yhwh, they placed a rich human leader at their head. Now, though, they realized that they lost their king because of their disobedience and Yhwh's power, and that their king could not defend them. At this point, it was clear that the king could not keep the people safe.

They still misunderstood the link between their trust in a king and their apostasy from Yhwh, however. Despite the words of this verse, their attitude did not change; they continued to worship the power they could see, instead of trusting Torah they heard. At first, when Yhwh did not seem to protect them enough, they wanted a king, so they could be like the other nations and keep themselves safe with a strong military leader. Yhwh told Samuel in 1 Sam 8 that he would give them a king because they rejected him.[11] Now in Hosea, the people mistakenly believed they lost their king because they did not fear Yhwh. In fact, they rejected Yhwh when they thought he could not defend them, then rejected their king when he showed weakness. The people respected the king because of his power—power which, in fact, he never possessed—and lost that respect when the king did not show power. The next time the people would be defeated, they would likely leave Yhwh and go back to a king.

Power meant more than Torah to the people, which Yhwh had to work to change. Once Yhwh would remove this king, they would have to learn that Yhwh did not ever approve of him—and this king *never* possessed power. The enemies whom the king supposedly defeated were defeated, in fact, by Yhwh's hand, and the invaders against whom this human failed to protect them overcame him by the same hand of Yhwh. Despite what they thought, when their king won, Yhwh remained in control, and when they lost, Yhwh was teaching them to return to Torah. Yhwh removed the king to prove the insanity of the people.

---

[11] 1 Sam 8:7-8.

V. 4 The people's inability to remain consistent would come out in judgment. The words they spoke were "empty oaths" because they promised to do one thing—remain loyal to Yhwh—while doing another—choosing a king for themselves and setting up altars and standing stones according to their own will. Their promises at the covenant proved empty.

Because they opposed the one who gives life, only weeds would come up in their fields. Weeds come from neglecting the fields, either because there is no seed or water or because the farmers are gone—dead or exiled. This state of their fields contrasted strongly with what we saw in ch. 2, where Yhwh supplied them with ample crops and riches (2:10; English 2:8). When the people diverted the bounty supplied by Yhwh and rejected its source, their prosperity ended.

V. 5 The ruin of the people of the Northern Kingdom came precisely from the source of their hope: their self-serving religion. The underlying sin of the people, for which they were sent into exile, was manifested when they mourned the destruction of their idol and religion rather than accept it as the will of Yhwh. Moreover, the priests so deeply invested themselves in this false system of trust that they still praised their idol even when Yhwh clearly and powerfully showed his superiority. Loyalty to power, not Yhwh, motivated them.

V. 6 Following their religion would bring more humiliation. The writer started out with "even it," to develop further the reference to the idol and its defeat in the previous verse. Yhwh gave the people riches, which they—beginning with the priests and princes—offered to the god of their hands.[12] Now this idol of

---

[12] We can think again of the idol in Exod 32:3, fashioned out of the people's gold and silver. Yhwh granted this gold and silver to the people by softening the heart of the

theirs ironically became a sacrifice to the enemy king, the "one who contends." The failure of their deity would bring them shame.

V. 7 The Samaritan king, allied with his deity, suffered the same defeat as the idol. The people originally demanded a king because they wanted a military leader to fight their battles for them. Even though Yhwh functioned as their military leader, as seen in Exod 14-15, they wanted a typical human leader, so they could be "like all the nations."[13] The defeat of their king at the hand of the Assyrian army showed that a human defender could simply be "mowed" down like grass by the superior force of Yhwh. They trusted one who had the staying power of a plant of the field. Their problem was not simply that they trusted in the wrong power, but that their reasoning was so impaired that a human king seemed to possess power.

V. 8 The source of the people's glory—as well as the indication of their rebelliousness—would become the source of their shame. The more they counted on their gods, priests, and king, the deeper the humiliation at their defeat. The priests would no longer tend the altars once the Assyrians took them away. Weeds would therefore take over the abandoned cultic space, twisting the priests' belief that the cult was the source of agricultural prosperity. Sin would force the people from the land and shame them because of the source of their pride. The higher the thistles, the longer and more permanent the defeat. The altars personified their shame, so they asked to be covered like the fallen Adam and Eve and to be buried by the earth itself.

Egyptians, despoiling them without a weapon. Their spoil became a sacrifice to the wrong god.

[13] 1 Sam 8:20.

V. 9 The people still sinned because they betrayed justice for the sake of self-preservation. The sin that the people committed now has not changed since the fratricidal war at Gibeah, which I explained in my commentary on ch. 5. Israelites "stood" at the war against Gibeah, whose residents raped the Levite's concubine to death. After victory against the Benjaminites, the other tribes of Israel continued to slaughter them. Defeating Benjamin's soldiers was not enough to make Israel feel safe. They had to destroy the tribe nearly completely before they felt they would not be overtaken.

When the people engaged in war, they brought shame upon themselves—even in victory. A sense of justice became self-righteous fury; the desire for victory turned into self-glorification by any means. Even when their leaders were successful in war, a war declared by Yhwh,[14] they still did not carry out Yhwh's teaching. War without loyalty ends in defeat, which underscored the people's betrayal.

V. 10 To instruct the people on how useless their deities and leaders were, Yhwh brought enemy peoples against them. To explain the *two* iniquities, we find a reference in 1 Kgs 12:26-30 to the *two* golden calves that Jeroboam established. The king even introduced them as the gods who brought them out of Egypt.[15]

A closer look at the Hebrew manuscript offers another way to read what I have translated "iniquities." While the Greek Septuagint interpreted this word as I did, the manuscript literally reads "eyes," while the medieval Masoretic marginal notes offer

---

[14] Judg 20:23.
[15] The Hebrew word is ambiguous, as we can translate it either as the proper name, "God," or a more generic, "gods."

"iniquities" as an alternate reading.[16] The people experienced Baal and Yhwh in distinct ways. A person sees an idol; one hears Yhwh. When one is bound to one's sense of sight, one is stuck with an idol. The sons of Israel, because they insisted on trusting in an idol, were bound to their two eyes and could no longer hear.

Hosea's audience was still bound by their two "eyes" to their two "iniquities," their calves, on the high places. At the precise moment when they trusted most strongly in their gods, Yhwh struck the object of their faith, to teach the rebellious people through their *ears* the futility of their professed "loyalty." Significantly, Yhwh attacked them via the nations, against whom Israel's gods were supposed to protect them.

V. 11 Yhwh proved through his teaching his mastery of the other so-called gods. He mocked Israel by depicting them as the bovines whose images they worship—whom he rides and drives.[17] Furthermore, Samaria's "bulls" were not glorious and to be worshiped, but common animals of labor, and the people were eager to work. Yhwh placed the yoke on the neck of his people: the North (Ephraim), the South (Judah), and the totality (Jacob). He would force them to act correctly through yoking them to his instruction.

The word for "who loves" looks peculiar in Hebrew, as I mentioned above in the text notes, but I read with the most common translation. The bare consonants spell, "I loved," but

---

[16] The difference between these two words in their written form is subtle. "Iniquity" is written עון and "eye" is עין. Even those not familiar with Hebrew can see that they only differ in the length of the middle letter. Confusion between these two letters occurs often in manuscripts.

[17] The Hebrew reinforces that they are female animals, as he addresses them in the second-person feminine, undermining the virility of their golden bulls.

with the vocalization as a feminine participle, the word ends with an extraneous final ׳ "yod." One would imagine that this word would be translated as, "I loved." The next clause, however, begins with an emphatic pronoun "I," which one would normally see before the first verb. It likely functions to contrast the subject of the previous clause. Finally, this verb could be read as a feminine second person, "you."[18] Normally, I would favor the consonants over the vowels, but in the current case, the emphatic pronoun unexpectedly appearing in the next clause tips me towards reading this as a feminine participle with an extraneous final ׳ "yod."

V. 12 The people had to work against character to prepare to receive Yhwh's teaching. With the assumption that the people were deeply broken, thus far incapable of remaining loyal to Yhwh, they had to toil in a new way. The second-person plural verbs commanded all the people to perform correct actions. To pass the paternity test, the offspring had to blossom resembling the Torah that Yhwh sowed.

The farming metaphors laid out the process, showing that both Yhwh and the people played a role in a good harvest. They sowed by ploughing the ground to receive the seed of righteousness. As the previous verse depicted the farmer, Yhwh, driving the oxen, the people, had to plough diligently under Yhwh's direction. When that ground was open, Yhwh sowed righteousness by casting the seed on them, so that they could consume the fruit that the plant produced. Then they could reap for themselves. In turn, they had the responsibility to manifest those fruits in acts of righteousness.[19]

---

[18] See Judg 5:7.
[19] Note the filled-out metaphor in Matt 13, Mark 4, and Luke 8.

The text equated the righteousness that Yhwh "casts" with his teaching by exploiting the double meaning of the verb in Hebrew. The root ירה, *YRH,* can mean both "cast" and "teach"; with the latter sense it is the root of the noun, תורה, *Torah.* Thus, we can also translate the last phrase, ". . . until he comes to teach righteousness to you." This further indicates that the people had to prepare themselves for a teaching, Yhwh's Torah, not for "righteousness" in an abstract or externally defined sense.

Note that the people "sow" and Yhwh "casts"; which one was performing the sowing action? Yhwh taught, so we would predict that Yhwh alone performed the action. Yhwh owned the seed, which is his teaching. The people prepared the ground, but they did not have anything to put in it. Practically, however, the action of "sowing" Torah required the people to read and hear Yhwh's Torah, by which action Yhwh sowed his teaching in their minds, typically referred to in Hebrew by the "heart." For example, we saw in ch. 4 that the priests were obliged to teach. By their teaching, Yhwh was teaching his Torah.

V. 13 We must read this verse as an antithesis to the previous one. Instead of sowing for righteousness, they plowed wickedness. They sowed not the seed that came from Yhwh, but the seed that they produced themselves. Instead of reaping for a mouth of loving-kindness, they reaped iniquity and ate the fruit of lies. Trusting in "warriors" stood apart as the main example of their disloyalty. It alone was expressed without a metaphor in this verse, rendering more concrete the nature of the metaphorical "seed" they were sowing. Instead of showing themselves to be sons of Yhwh, they, as sons of Baal, trusted themselves and their warriors.

Moreover, the other verbs address the collective of the community in the second-person plural, while the verb "you trusted" is in the singular. In this way, the prophecy narrowed on the king. In the first half of the verse, the prophet used the plural to address how the people plowed, reaped, and ate the fruit of wickedness. The prophet addressed the king in the singular in the second half of the verse, telling him that he trusted in his own ways and his warriors. The people's dedication to wicked deeds crystalized in the king's misplaced trust in his military.

While the addressee would most likely be the king originally, later hearers should hear the accusation of disloyalty leveled at them, despite not sitting on the literal throne. That way, the metaphorical farming actions addressed Ephraim generally, but this final accusation points the finger directly and abruptly at the hearer. The hearer, beholden to his own conscience, wants to secure him- or herself rather than seek Yhwh as a father and protector.

V. 14 No matter how powerful the army, or how strong the fortifications, a force from Yhwh could overwhelm any of them. The king used so much of his wealth—the substance of the people—to defend himself and (at least ostensibly) the people, but nothing would come of it. The city would be destroyed until all the citizens, even the women and children, would be killed. The defenses would be shown to be no defense at all against Yhwh's might. Hence, the name of the location destroyed is "Beit Arav-El," meaning, "The House of the Ambush of God."

The king's plan opposed Yhwh as the only defender of the people. The author laid out the answer to the people's question in v. 3. They saw that their king was removed because they did not trust Yhwh. Their king and priests deluded themselves and followed their own ways so that their gods and their warriors could defend them against "Shalman," who functioned as Yhwh's agent to perform what he promised in v. 10. While this name may well refer to Shalmaneser, King of Assyria, it ironically contains the root of the word for peace, "shalom." The ambush and destruction of the city and of the people confirmed their powerlessness as Yhwh established his own "shalom" as he destroyed what his people had set up.

V. 15 Bethel represented a shrine for Israelite devotion, where they believed they were worshiping Yhwh. As we have seen, the people's worship of Yhwh proved empty, because they refused to follow his teaching. They only thought they were worshiping Yhwh. They trusted that their empty religious gestures would ensure their safety with Yhwh, but Yhwh wanted only loyalty, not empty gestures. The "wickedness of their wickedness" was the emptiness of their empty rites.

Hosea underscored the end of the kingship that the people relied on for their false sense of safety. The final verb for "cut off"—repeated twice for emphasis in Hebrew—reprises the same verb "cut off" used in v. 7 for the King of Samaria. Just as the latter king was eliminated along with the idol, so now the King of Israel was utterly cut off, bookending and reiterating that the king would be destroyed. In the context of the end of the last chapter, the people and king and idol would all be destroyed in this war.

Israel's defeat caused by Yhwh

The coming of Assyria revealed the emptiness of the people's paradigm for defense, by taking their idol, priest, and king into exile. The shame did not come simply because of their defeat, but because the judgment would show them how wrong they were. Yhwh would prove to them that their fealty to him was all talk with no action; moreover, their actions revealed that they in fact placed their trust in their own army and fortifications, undermining their religious piety as perfunctory.

At this point the prophet challenged the people to act correctly, accepting Yhwh as the bringer of good and bad. They must follow Torah as Yhwh's teaching. All prosperity came from his hand—the same hand from which came the current threat of exile. For this test, the people only had to answer one question: *Will you accept suffering at the hand of Yhwh?* If so, they would return as Yhwh's sons to carry out Torah in their actions; if not, they would turn back to serve their king and Baal, their true father, who they thought would defend them and provide them food again. Based on historical precedent, unfortunately, Israel did not have a chance of choosing well.

Chapter 11

¹ *When Israel was a boy, I loved him; from Egypt I called him my son.*

² *They called to them, so they went from before them. To the Baals they used to sacrifice, and to the images they used to burn incense.*

³ *I taught Ephraim to walk,¹ taking them on my arms.² And they did not know that I healed them.*

⁴ *With cords of a man I drew them, with ropes of love. I was like those who raise the yoke on their cheeks that I might stretch out to him and feed him.³*

---

¹ This verb, תרגלתי, *tirgaltî*, is a peculiar form, as it looks like a Hiphil in the suffixing conjugation, but with a unique t- prefix. While this could represent the unique instance of a separate conjugation, I choose to read this as a Hiphil, "I made to walk."

Wilhelm Gesenius claimed that it is a denominative form from a rare form *Tiphel* (*Taphel*). The analogies do not share precisely the same form, however (Hebrew Grammar, ed. E. Kautsch, trans. A. E. Cowley, Second English Edition [Oxford: Clarendon Press, 1910], §55h).

² The Masoretic Text reads עַל־זְרוֹעֹתָיו, *'al-zero'otav*, "on his arms." The Septuagint reads ἀνέλαβον αὐτὸν ἐπὶ τὸν βραχίονά μου, which implies that the final "waw" of the Masoretic Text was a duplication of the following letter through scribal error. Hence, I am reading it, עַל־זְרוֹעֹתַי, *'al-zero'otay*, without the final "waw."

³ With *Biblia Hebraica Stuttgartensia* I read the לֹא (לוֹ), *lô*, at the end of this verse, even though it appears at the beginning of the next verse in the Masoretic Text.

The switch from plural to singular ("they" to "it") comes as the metaphor shifts. The author was writing about Ephraim in the plural, but the move to the singular signaled a return to the original metaphor of the people as a single son. This same son continues in the next verse as the one who acts.

⁵He will return to the land of Egypt; Assyria is his king, because they refused to turn back.⁴

⁶The sword will whirl in his cities and will make an end of his branches and will devour them because of their counsels.

⁷My people are bent on apostatizing from me, yet they call him "God Most High." They will not exalt together.⁵

⁸How will I give you up, O Ephraim? protect you, O Israel? How will I make you like Admah, set you like Zeboyim? My heart is turned against me, my changes of heart are warmed together.

⁹I will not carry out⁶ the heat of my anger; I will not turn to destroy Ephraim, for I am a god and not a man, the holy one in your midst, and I will not come into the city.

¹⁰After Yhwh they will walk. He will roar like a lion, for he will roar, and sons will tremble from the West.

¹¹They tremble like a bird from Egypt and like a dove from the land of Assyria, and I shall settle them on their houses, oracle of Yhwh.⁷

---

[4] Again, we see some slippage between Israel as a collective of individuals ("they") and as a metaphorical son ("he").

[5] The references changed from first- to third-person because the god whom the people worshipped was a different entity from the god who was speaking.

[6] Lit. "do."

[7] English 11:12 appears as 12:1 in Hebrew. Thus, I will discuss that verse as part of the next chapter.

Chapter 11

Yhwh's inner logic

This chapter pays special attention to the actions of Yhwh. Chapters 4-10 depicted from multiple angles the betrayal and apostasy of the people, but now we turn to the deep difference between human and divine loyalty. Yhwh's loyal nature highlighted even more strongly the people's self-interested, short-sighted inconstancy.

Yhwh defined himself here as the one-and-only father. He reared Israel as his son, never wavering from his duty. From Israel's birth, childhood, and rebellious adolescence, he taught them, never neglecting them for a moment. Israel's childhood represents an important theme, not for its own sake or for the mere sentiment of "childhood." The earliest part of the story testified that Yhwh took care of them, as he taught them to walk and to work.

Tension would arise because they would find themselves exiled and destroyed—apparently abandoned by Yhwh. In fact, Israel constantly abandoned their god in spite of Yhwh's faithfulness. When they abandoned him, he allowed them to follow another king and enslave themselves. While he acted for their good, he let them act against their own self-interest. Outside of his protection, they were vulnerable to their enemies, just as when they found themselves in Egypt before he brought them to himself.

Even in these dire straits, Yhwh would not give up on them. He still promised hope. In the end, he was merciful because what he did for the first generation—even after they abandoned him—he would do for the next generation. As he brought his son out of Egypt, he would bring the next generation home from Assyria.

* * *

This chapter elaborated on the paternity test set up in chs. 1-3 by developing the relationship of father and son. As I said in my comments on ch. 1, the one to whom they showed loyalty would determine their true paternity. In the present chapter, Yhwh depicted how he raised the people as his son, teaching them from the first day. The author contrasted the tenderness of the early days, when Yhwh acted as their true father, with the near-immediate betrayal of Israel, who acted as if he no longer was. Yhwh could pass the paternity test, even if the people could not.

One could read the seemingly emotional restating of the past in this chapter as evidence of Yhwh's sentimentality, but we saw him reject his feelings to come to his conclusion. He was of two minds, whether to preserve or destroy his people. But he chose *against* his emotion, the bitterness of betrayal, and preserved them. Yhwh remained bound to his duty as father to the people.

Egypt functioned as a paradigm to understand how Assyria would reprise the Exodus story.[8] First, Assyria posed the danger of "Egyptian" enslavement. The people inside the story hearing the prophet's words would experience the same slavery in Assyria as their ancestors did in Egypt. Second, "Egypt" referred to the state of servitude as Israel imposed it on themselves in their own country when they abandoned Yhwh. Third, Egypt was Israel's "womb" from which they were born. As Yhwh brought them out of Egypt as his son, he would return them to their homes after Assyria.

Commentary

V. 1 From Israel's beginning Yhwh presented his loyalty consistently. Throughout the Book of Hosea, the writer

---

[8] I discussed the connection between Egypt and Assyria first in ch. 7, and again in ch. 9.

referenced the Exodus as the beginning of Israel's nationhood. In the current verse, the preposition "from" can also be translated "since," and so pointed to the *place* from which Yhwh called Israel and to the *moment* he called them. Yhwh's fatherhood began from Egypt in both respects, as the "boy's" birth occurred as he came out of Egypt. The people's slavery under Pharaoh ended as they came under Yhwh's aegis, once he took them as his own.

This event established Yhwh's fatherhood in the context of the paternity test that the people were being scrutinized for since the beginning of Hosea. "Calling" him his son used the language of adoption, which subverted the "biological" paternity of Yhwh. The author added virtue to Yhwh by emphasizing that he took on this boy, Israel, as a son, even though Yhwh may not have sired him. The prophet's word tested the paternity of the people, as it established Yhwh's potential paternity based on their actions.

V. 2 Israel heard more than one voice. Just as Yhwh "called" them his son, the Baals "called" to them.[9] While the Baals were not defined at the beginning of the verse, the following clause showed that Israel followed the Baals. The writer left ambiguous who actually called (other gods? their leaders? their own hearts?), but Israel's actions proved that they heard the Baals.

They followed the teaching of the Baals immediately. They performed the correct cultic rites towards them with sacrifices and incense. Yet the Baals did not show any care in return. At this point, all blessings clearly came from Yhwh—including their very existence as a people. Their actions, unfortunately, showed that they looked to the Baals as their fathers.

---

[9] Hebrew uses the same word for "call," קרא, *qara'*, in both instances.

V. 3 Although Israel soon wandered from Yhwh, he continued to raise them. He taught them to walk, acting as a father. Yhwh expected the people not just to pronounce loyalty to him but more importantly to act according to his will as his children. Whether or not he was the "biological" father of the people, his actions showed him to be so. Moreover, he healed them when they were in need.

Teaching to walk and bearing on his arms in this context referred to the Exodus. Once Yhwh called his son from Egypt, he took care of him. Despite the Israelites' quick apostasy in the מדבר, *midbar*, "wilderness," he healed this deep sickness of theirs. Granted, they apostatized again many times afterwards, but Yhwh healed them by opening the possibility of coming back.

V. 4 Yhwh referred again to the people as a work animal, as we saw in 10:11. This image illustrated the expectations of the people, that they work according to Yhwh's will and that Yhwh would train them.

By our modern standards, the image of the master controlling an ox does not seem tender enough to coincide with the loving father. A worker drives his beasts to work for his benefit, and he keeps them healthy and alive insofar as they can serve him. Servitude in v. 4 stands in tension with tenderness in vv. 1 and 3.

Yet Yhwh, the owner of the beast, treated his oxen with unusual kindness. He pulled them with ropes of a "human" and of "love." He even lifted the yoke up from their neck, so he could feed them from his own hand. While the beast served, this owner pulled gently and lightened the burden. Combined with the reference to the beasts of burden in 10:11, the farmer drove his animals to work, but gently. Yhwh wanted to teach Israel to learn to follow his will and serve him, where he could treat them with exceeding mercy.

In addition, the metaphor of an ox played with the image of the golden bulls that represented Baal. While those who worshiped Baal created and bowed down to images of an ox to serve them, Yhwh referred to the people as the ox over whom he was the master.

V. 5 At this verse, the frame shifted from the origins of Israel in Egyptian slavery to their new Assyrian slavery. The people did not need to return to the land of Egypt to find themselves in the slavery of Egypt. In my comments on 7:11 and 16, 8:13, and ch. 9, I showed that Egypt functioned as a metaphor for the state of slavery. "Egyptian" slavery would exist again when they would be taken away to Assyria. While they would not return to geographical Egypt, they would serve the king of Assyria just as they served Pharaoh.

Even before they were led captive to Assyria, Israel placed themselves under bondage because they did not want to turn to follow Yhwh. Their betrayal of Yhwh kept them from his gentle rule and turned them to a harsh, Egyptian slavery.

More specifically in the current context, the people turned to Egypt for assistance when Assyria threatened them seriously. Elsewhere in the Bible, the King of Assyria charged that King Hezekiah of Judah counted on Egypt for protection (2 Kgs 18:21). Scripture thus depicted Judah as having placed themselves under Egyptian military defense, which required servitude. A new Pharaoh dictated these Israelites' moves and demanded loyalty. In return, he provided at best the minimum for survival. The Israelites performed every act demanded of them out of fear of losing this so-called protection. Foreign powers and gods exerted this control even in the Israelites' homeland. The people thus turned from one master to another, all while snubbing Yhwh.

Since King Sennacherib defeated Egypt, as we can see in historical records as well as in the biblical story, Israel could not come out free because they would not return to Yhwh. The text plays on the Hebrew verb שוב, *shûb*, "turn, return; repent," because Israel will "shub" to the land of Egypt because they refused to "shub" toward Yhwh.

King Hezekiah was fickle. In the account in 2 Kgs 18:7, King Hezekiah remained faithful, depending on Yhwh, who favored him. In vv. 11-12, Assyria defeated the Northern Kingdom because they did not follow "the covenant, everything his servant, Moses, commanded." As Assyria turned against Judah, though, Hezekiah submitted to Assyria, asking for concessions and paying them off with the riches of the temple (vv. 14-16). According to the accusations of the Assyrians against Judah, the latter also trusted in Egypt for help. One moment he trusted in Yhwh, but under pressure, sought help from both Assyria and Egypt. Hezekiah found himself only for a short time "turning" back to Yhwh before he "turned" back to earthly armies and their physical strength.

V. 6 The teaching they followed determined their fate, for following something besides Torah would lead to their destruction. The juxtaposition of "counsels" is surprising, because one would expect the foreign swords, chariots, or armies to have caused the destruction of their cities. Counsels, though, destroyed them. In other words, the sword would come to them from the King of Assyria—via invasion—because of the teaching they followed. The worldly "counsel" of navigating the politics of

Chapter 11

Assyria and Egypt for the sake of safety contradicted the teaching of trusting in Yhwh, the lone method of their salvation.

V. 7 The actions—or lack thereof—of the people corroborated that their prayers were lip-service to Yhwh. The reader should note how the people turned from "me," referring to Yhwh, but instead called "him," their other god, "God Most High." While they called up to their deity, they did not act as if Yhwh was on high. The people thought they were calling to Yhwh, when their actions attested that they called to some other god. All their words did not praise Yhwh at all.

"El," which I translated as "God," could have two meanings. I translated it as another name for Yhwh, but it could also be the proper name of Baal's father in Canaanite mythology, rendering the phrase, "El Most High." Either meaning pointed to apostasy because the matter was their actions, not their words. Whether Israel besought their god, Yhwh, or the Most High Father of Baal, their actions showed no loyalty to Yhwh. The god they turned to could not pull them out of their problems, the very reason why they needed to call to him.

V. 8 Yhwh did not give up on taking care of them, and so remained faithful to his initial responsibility as father. Before we understand the dynamics of Yhwh's dilemma, however, we must recall the role of Admah and Zeboyim. They were allies of Sodom and Gomorrah against Chedorlaomer in Gen 14, and they were destroyed along with the two cities by Yhwh in Gen 19:28, according to Deut 29:22 (English, Deut 29:23).

Yhwh had to decide whether to preserve Israel, in spite of their habitual apostasy, or destroy them because of it. On the one hand, he wanted to protect them as a father would protect his children. On the other hand, they deserved the punishment that Sodom and Gomorrah—along with Admah and Zeboyim—endured because of their wickedness. He had to weigh the two logical reactions to Israel's rebellion.

These place names bear additional meanings in Hebrew that clarify Yhwh's agenda against the cities that the humans built to protect themselves. "Admah" means "earth, ground," and "Zeboyim," "(the place of) hyenas." Hebrew does not have capital letters to distinguish common from proper nouns, so the phrase can equally be translated, "How will I make you like earth and set you like the place of hyenas?" In other words, Yhwh threatened to remove civilization completely, rendering Israel an open land where shepherds would feel at home, rather than a city for the wealthy to prosper by their own hand.[10]

Even though Yhwh could not give up his duty and memory of those first actions he took on Israel's behalf, he remained of two minds. He became angry, and then merciful, and so his "changes of heart" or his mercies remained heated inside him. He did not change his relationship with them, even though he changed his tactics, from mercy to wrath and back.

V. 9 Yhwh continued to describe his internal state as he determined the best course of action. He decided not to act on his anger to destroy Ephraim altogether, even though they earned that response. His reaction was divine. The story of Gilead and the Benjaminites comes to mind again, even though it was not mentioned in this text, because of their overwrought, violent, typically human response to being betrayed. Yhwh refused to

---

[10] "Zeboyim" could also come from the word "(the place of) gazelles." This would not change the main point, however. Gazelles thrive in the uncivilized wilderness, as well.

overreact because he was "a god and not a man." He remained the only trace of holiness in their midst—manifested by his Torah.

While one might think it would be good if Yhwh were to enter into and dwell in the city, this verse made such a visit sound bad. Yet he promised to be in their "midst." We must note that the context suggested that "I will not come into" and "I will not turn to destroy Ephraim" likely referred to the same action. If he came into the city, his anger would surely destroy it. Nevertheless, he would remain among them as his holy teaching, even if they went into exile. The desire was for the teaching to dwell among the people, not the deity in the city. He chose not to destroy and remove the city from the ground—yet.

V. 10 The story shifted from the present generation of listeners to the next one. The teaching and its manifestation in the exile would be a strong message to its future audience. The people would one day walk after the ways of Yhwh by following his teaching. The fierce wrath he expressed in the exile would become their teaching. The "sons," the children of the witnesses of the exile, would tremble when they heard the story of Yhwh's actions on their forefathers. The "West" represented the land where the remnant resided—the sons either of those who went into exile and returned, or of those few who never left. The ones who trembled at Yhwh's word and acted accordingly would be "sons" of Yhwh's Torah; they would pass the paternity test.

V. 11 The author imagined a silly, flitting bird[11] who bobs from one home to another and inserted Yhwh as the one who could take care of it. The people were defenseless as they searched for help from Assyria and Egypt, since neither could defend them, so

---

[11] For other examples, see 4:19; 7:11; 9:8, 11.

they had nothing left but to tremble in fear. At that point, Yhwh returned to his role as savior and defender and found a safe home for them. When they depended on Yhwh to take care of them, he would do so, as he had done from the beginning. As he brought one generation out of Egypt into the מדבר, *midbar,* "wilderness," and their children from the מדבר, *midbar,* into the Land, so he would settle the next generation after Assyrian exile.[12]

Faithful from beginning to end

If the next generation should maintain Yhwh's teaching in their midst and tremble at the teaching that would come from the Assyrian exile, they might experience hope. As Yhwh would roar and *the sons* would hear him *from the West,* we see the root of the plan. They would be the children of those who were not exiled, hearers of the story from the mouths of those who witnessed Yhwh's wrath. The witnesses must announce the wrath, however, in order for the next generation to have hope. Their testimony would encourage the children to follow Yhwh's teaching.

This god knew how to create a people, and he may need to do so again. The people would be exiled to Assyria, very much like their forefathers in Egypt. As the people put themselves in "Egypt" again by submitting to earthly kings, Yhwh may need to bring them out of "Egypt" again to create a people. Instead of a Torah from Sinai this time, Torah would come from Assyria, a teaching about Yhwh's wrath and salvation.

The next generation must learn from the judgment against their forefathers. Yhwh was always more than a willing, generous father;

---

[12] This verse ends with "oracle of Yhwh," which sets ch. 1-11 off from the last three chapters. The only other time that we saw this phrase in Hosea was in 2:15, 18, 23 (English 2:13, 16, 21).

he never stopped his desire to help and save them, even when they rejected him. They only had to stop listening to the ones who "called" them and to listen exclusively to Yhwh's teaching. Then they could follow it to avoid the tragedy their forefathers lived through.

Chapter 12

¹Ephraim surrounded me with lies, and the house of Israel with rebellion. Judah still wandered with a god, and with holy ones he is secure.¹

²Ephraim is a shepherd of wind and a pursuer of the East wind; all day long he multiplies falsehood and destruction. A covenant with Assyria they cut, and oil they bear for Egypt.²

³Yhwh has a dispute with Judah, and it will be visited upon Jacob according to his ways, and according to his deeds he will turn it upon him.

⁴In the womb he took his brother by the heel, and by his strength he contended with God.

⁵And he contended with the angel and defeated him; he cried and entreated him for mercy. He found him at Bethel, and there he was speaking with him.

⁶Yhwh, the god of hosts, Yhwh is his memorial.

⁷And you will return to your god. Keep kindness and justice, and hope in your god forever.

⁸A merchant: his scales of deceit are in his hand; he loves to oppress.

---

[1] This is 11:12 in English.
[2] This is 12:1 in English.

⁹And Ephraim said, "How I became rich! I found strength for myself! As for all my toil, they will not find in me iniquity that is sin."

¹⁰But I am Yhwh, your god from the land of Egypt. I will still settle you in tents like the days of the tent of meeting.

¹¹I spoke to the prophets, and I myself multiplied a vision; by the hand of the prophets I will silence them.

¹²Is Gilead iniquity? Indeed, they were false. In Gilgal they slaughtered oxen. Indeed, their altars are like heaps in the furrows of my fields.

¹³And Jacob fled to the field of Aram, and Israel served for a woman, and for a woman he kept sheep.

¹⁴And by a prophet Yhwh brought up Israel from Egypt, and by a prophet he was kept.

¹⁵Ephraim caused bitter anger, so his lord will leave his blood on him and return his reproach to him.

Two origin histories

This chapter juxtaposes two origin stories of Israel to further Yhwh's argument from the previous chapter, namely, that he has consistently cared for Israel since their "birth," despite their unfaithfulness. In ch. 11, Yhwh argued that he never abandoned them, even when they turned away from him. In ch. 12, Yhwh furthered his argument by recalling biblical events where the people led themselves into slavery and suffering when left on their own but were led into safety and security by his hand.

Torah presented two origin stories for Israel. The first comes from Gen 25-35: the story of Jacob-Israel, the patriarch and namesake of the people. The second, but perhaps most famous, that of salvation from Pharaoh, comes from Exod 1-15.

A few scenes from the life of Jacob-Israel bring particular importance for this chapter in Hosea. This patriarch took from his brother, sold himself into slavery, and fought against Yhwh. Jacob, that is, "Supplanter," supplanted his brother, Esau, in the womb and snatched away his birthright. He later left the land for Aram, served his uncle for fourteen years because of his love of Rachel, and struggled with the angel of Yhwh (Gen 25-32). This final struggle culminated in the angel changing his name to "Israel," that is, "He Struggles with God," formally establishing contention as his identity (32:28). Genesis reprised this name change when God told Jacob to build an altar to him, who saved him from the wrath of his brother, and Jacob turned fulfilling God's command into an act of literal idolatry (35:10-14). Hence, Jacob-Israel embedded in the core of his being contention against God and his brother.

The second origin story is the Exodus from Egypt, and we already saw Hosea depend on this event for his narrative. Israel became a people when Yhwh brought them out of slavery to give them his Torah by the hand of Moses. Yhwh claimed Israel as his son "out of Egypt" (Hos 11:1). Once in the wilderness, however, the people rebelled as they discovered and bowed down to the Baals (Hos 11:2). Elsewhere, Hosea referred to this adoption as first finding their fathers "in the wilderness (מדבר, *midbar*)" (Hos 9:10).

Hosea thus presented two ways of "being Israel": one where they fought against Yhwh to follow their own will, and one where Yhwh made them as his people. Between these opposing views, following Yhwh continued to be the logical, prosperous path.

Hence, Hosea exhorted his hearer to submit to the will of Yhwh, who would provide them the prosperity they enjoyed before.

Excursus: Jacob's rebellious "pillar" in Genesis 35

We often assume that Jacob-Israel, the patriarch of the people of Israel, was a "good guy." The biblical text does not necessarily bear this assumption out. In the midst of Hosea 12:3-7, we saw Jacob-Israel depicted, on the contrary, as overreaching and rebellious. This raised the question of whether *we* are forcing an interpretation of Jacob-Israel against the texts of Genesis or if *Hosea* is.

On the surface, Genesis appeared to depict Jacob-Israel in multiple ways. The renaming of "Jacob" as "Israel" occurred twice in Genesis, in chs. 32 and 35. As mentioned above, Gen 32 presented Jacob as rebellious, struggling with God.[3] In Gen 35, however, Jacob appeared to obey God. On the surface, the two events contradicted each other.

When one looks more deeply at the latter event, however, one observes a subtle but consistent trait of rebelliousness. At first, Jacob appeared to follow his god's will. In v. 1, God told Jacob to build an altar, and, in v. 3, Jacob dutifully replied to his household that he would build an altar to God, as he confiscated all the foreign gods in their midst in v. 4. God rewarded his words of obedience by keeping him safe from enemies surrounding him in v. 5, so Jacob built the altar at Bethel in v. 7.

The blessing from the God of Jacob carried rebellion ironically at its core. At this point, Jacob did not struggle against him, yet God pronounced in the next verses the "blessing" of Jacob's name-

---

[3] In Gen 32 and 35 the author never referred to the deity as "Yhwh" (often translated as "Lord"), but only as "God" (*[ha]Elohim*).

change with a surprising reminder to Jacob that he struggled against God (35:9-10). During the first verses, Jacob's actions reflected strong obedience, and in 35:9, God blessed him. The next verse reiterated the name-change from Gen 32, which we normally associate with Jacob's wrestling match against his god. If the name-change embedded rebellion in Jacob's identity, why did the ch. 35 text reiterate this renaming right after Jacob showed his obedience? What function did the name change play here?

After establishing the altar, Jacob disobeyed, even if it appears at first glance that he complied. Jacob seemed to add to his virtue by complementing his altar with a pillar in v. 14, dedicating it to the god who spoke to him by calling it "Beth-El," that is, "House of God." The text stressed this point by repetition: "So Jacob set up a pillar in the place where he spoke with him, a pillar of stone" (Gen 35:14a).

The author depicted the objects built by Jacob with polarizing terms, as altars and pillars are very different objects. An altar, מזבח, *mizbêax*, can be positive. For example, in the competition between the Prophet Elijah and the prophets of Baal in 1 Kgs 18, each side built an altar (מזבח, *mizbêax*) to its god, and Yhwh was victorious when he devoured the burnt offering. Moreover, Yhwh accepted Noah's sacrifice from his מזבח, *mizbêax* (Gen 8:20-21). Most significantly, Yhwh commanded that a מזבח, *mizbêax*, be built in the tabernacle in the wilderness (Exod 20:24-25). A few other texts, however, depicted a מזבח, *mizbêax*, as negative.[4]

In contrast, Yhwh made strong imprecations against preserving a "pillar," a מצבה, *matstsebâ*, or alternatively, מצבת, *matstsebeth*.

---

[4] We saw a negative example of a מזבח, *mizbêax*, built for the people to perpetuate their prosperity in Hos 10:1-2. See also Deut 12:3.

In general, a מצבה, *matstsebâ*, carried the same status as a graven image; the second iteration of the Ten Commandments includes this term among forbidden objects (Lev 26:1; Deut 7:5). Elsewhere, Yhwh pronounced hatred against them (Deut 16:22), and several texts depicted kings as virtuous because they tore down a מצבה, *matstsebâ* (Hezekiah in 2 Kgs 18:4; Josiah in 2 Kgs 23:14).[5]

Significantly, Hosea depicted these pillars earlier as creations that expressed the wrong conception of prosperity. As in my remarks on 10:1-2, the people misunderstood the prosperity Yhwh provided, and used it to create cultic objects—both a מצבה, *matstsebâ*, and a מזבח, *mizbêax*—to grab more. The false hope in their ability to preserve prosperity would prove false when they failed to protect themselves.

The reprise of Jacob's name-change in Gen 35 after Jacob showed his obedience, reminded Jacob of and judged him for his penchant for rebellion, which he immediately confirmed. God commanded Jacob to build a מזבח, *mizbêax*—not a מצבה, *matstsebâ*. Jacob began obedient, by building the former. Then Yhwh warned Jacob-Israel of the rebellion embedded in his name, which Jacob-Israel followed on by building a מצבה, *matstsebâ*, against God's dislike of this cultic object. Verse 35:14 underscored Jacob's willful, rebellious action by not mentioning it only once, but by repeating "a מצבת, *matstsebeth*, of stone." He built precisely what, during the course of the biblical narrative, Yhwh

---

[5] While we never find a good מצבה, *matstsebâ*, we find two examples used with a neutral sense. Moses set up twelve, representing the twelve tribes of Israel (Exod 24:4). Isaiah spoke of a מזבח, *mizbêax*, and a מצבה, *matstsebâ*, dedicated to Yhwh in Egypt (Isa 19:19). In neither case was a negative word or consequence spoken.

announced he despised, and what manifested the people's rejection of Yhwh in 1-2 Kings, the very items Kings Hezekiah and Josiah had to bring down. Jacob-Israel confirmed the judgment of his name when he expressed his self-will through idolatry. The nature of the father had been passed down to all the children of Israel.

As in the sins of Jezreel and Gibeah, Jacob-Israel overstepped their bounds, misled by corrupt piety. Jehu wiped out the royal family at Jezreel because the prophet went beyond the words he was commanded to recite. The war from Gibeah began because the people were correct to act, but exceeded their mandate when they attempted genocide. It was not enough for Jacob-Israel to build a מזבח, *mizbêax*; he had to add on an idolatrous מצבה, *matstsebâ*. Fulfilling Yhwh's commandment in simple obedience did not suffice in the corrupt thinking of the people.

Commentary

V. 1 The entire house of Israel—Ephraim and Judah—compulsively rejected Yhwh and followed other gods. The verse here uses אל, *'el,* which can mean either a generic "god" or El, the father of Baal. I explained that the same ambiguity in Hos 11:7 indicated either way that the people were unfaithful. Furthermore, the word "secure" comes from the same root as "trust," אמן, *'MN.*[6] They followed the chief of the Canaanite pantheon as well as the divine beings, the "holy ones," around him.

V. 2 The work put into following other gods and kings bore no fruit. Attempting to shepherd wind required a lot of work with no result. Ephraim focused their strength into the wrong areas, and, as a result, were destroyed. Their effort was expended on the

---

[6] This is the same root as אמת, *'emet,* "truth." See discussion on verse 4:1.

surrounding powers, whom they chose to appease. Between the agreement with Assyria and the service to Egypt, they believed they made good investments with their time and energy. Yhwh reminded them numerous times, however, that the work would not pay off; these superpowers could not defend them.

V. 3 Yhwh wanted to make a case against Israel. We saw this case unfold over the last few chapters: Yhwh consistently acted faithfully with the people and they did not trust him, thereby betraying him countless times. Even though he offered them a teaching that would give them life, they suffered. The situation threatened to get worse because of the choice they made to reject him and his teaching, and to accept the teaching of other gods and powers. They finally chose against Yhwh and for their own power, even resorting to fratricide.

The author referred here to the people in specific and unusual ways that specified their transgressions. When he referred to "Judah," he pointed at the division between the two parts of the kingdom. Judah's king sinned when an attack from the Northern Kingdom seemed imminent. King Ahaz of Judah made deals with Assyria so the neighbors to the North would not conquer them (2 Kgs 16).[7]

One would expect the totality of the people to be referred to as "Israel," but here we find "Jacob." The Hebrew word "Jacob" means, "he supplants, takes by the heal," and highlights this trait of the son of Isaac who supplanted his brother. (See more on this in the next verse.) As Israel tried to defeat his brother Judah, the war resulted in Judah siding with a foreign power against his

---

[7] Predictably, the narrator condemned King Ahaz for worshiping other gods (2 Kgs 16:3-4, 10-18).

brother. Fratricide lay at the center as one brother tried to supplant the other's power.

V. 4 Jacob's initial selfishness and self-determination began the argument, based on his name. Hosea played on the two names of Jacob-Israel by using them as the verbs of this verse. "Took by the heal" uses the same root as "Jacob," and "contended with God," derives from the same root שרה, *SRH,* "contend (with)," as the name "Israel." In two clauses, the prophet alluded to the two willful incidents for which this patriarch was named. Israel was the one who fought willfully from the beginning, taking what he wanted from his brother and his god.

V. 5 It is difficult to follow the participants in this verse because of the pronouns; none of the subjects or direct objects are named except one. I am interpreting the pronouns this way: "And Jacob contended with the angel, and Jacob defeated the angel; the angel cried, and the angel entreated Jacob for mercy. Jacob found the angel at the House of God, and there Jacob was speaking with the angel."

Yhwh's contention continued with the struggle between Jacob and the angel of Yhwh. Jacob would not let the angel go until the angel blessed him, even when the angel told Jacob to let him go. The angel, therefore, renamed Jacob, "Israel" (Gen 32:24-32). On another occasion, Yhwh was speaking with Jacob at Bethel and said that Jacob's name would no longer be Jacob, but Israel (Gen 35:9-15). Significantly, Jacob did not act correctly in either instance, as I explained in the excursus (above), which paralleled the people's behavior as described in Hosea. Jacob-Israel, like the people of his namesake, fought against Yhwh, and worshiped him according to their own will.

V. 6 Two competing histories of Israel exist: the one that their forefather, Jacob began, and the one that Yhwh began. The previous verses described the former. When their forefather acted, he followed his own will. He forced his way into supplanting his brother, and he refused to submit to God or his angel. He ended up enslaving himself out of the land for his wife, and then brought his whole family out of the land to be enslaved in Egypt. The people of his name, Israel, followed in his footsteps to slavery.

In this verse, Yhwh offered another, contrasting history—from which he formed the foundation and potential "memorial" for the next generation. He showed that he could free his people from Egyptian slavery and give them prosperity in the land if they were willing to submit to his Torah. By carrying out his commandments the people could live in the land securely, without enslaving themselves to domestic or foreign kings or any other god. His name should be a memory forever. They could leave a legacy of peace to their children if Yhwh, and his deeds in the Exodus, remained their memorial.

V. 7 The prophet offered a plan for success. As long as the people followed Torah through acts of kindness and justice, they showed hope in their god, that they might continue to enjoy prosperity at his hand. This result proved that they returned to Yhwh. These concrete actions displayed their "hope," that is, trust.

V. 8 The lifestyle opposed to kindness consists of acting unjustly. The rich merchant, who cheats his customers with false balances and oppresses those weaker than him, epitomizes this conduct. The prophet thus presented a dichotomy in vv. 7-8: act generously and mercifully or cheat and oppress others. When the people returned to and hoped in Yhwh, as the previous verse described, the people did not fear a lack of prosperity. They trusted Yhwh.

Chapter 12

When they believed they needed to provide for themselves, they took from whomever they could.

V. 9 Following the previous verse, Ephraim proved which road they were on: the road of oppression. Wealth excited them, and they explicitly claimed that they got it for *themselves* and that it came thanks to *their* toil. They did not ascribe their prosperity to Yhwh. They believed that they accomplished it without sin, but they showed that they could not have done so otherwise. "Sin" did not consist of committing this or that action but was rebelling against Yhwh as the only provider. The fact that they bragged of their prosperity and ascribed it to themselves displayed their sin. Their ignorant statement betrayed a fundamental lie, that they could make themselves rich and still submit to Yhwh and his Torah.

V. 10 Yhwh needed to start over because the people acted like they had never heard of Torah, so they required a return to the מדבר, *midbar*, "wilderness," their other beginning—and their initiation into Yhwh's instruction at Sinai. Some other teaching was lodged in them, as if they just came out of hundreds of years in Egypt. He reminded the people in this verse again, like in 11:1, that he was their god since he brought them out of Egypt. At that point the relationship began with Yhwh overseeing them and taking care of them.

Settling the people in tents bore a double meaning. First, it recalled Israel's beginnings, when they received Torah in Sinai and all of them dwelt in tents. Even Yhwh resided in the tent of meeting. Second, Yhwh was threatening the end of their cities and a return to pastoral life for their entire country.

This verse also fulfilled Yhwh's promise in 2:16-17, wherein he would "allure" his wife into the מדבר, *midbar*, "wilderness," where he could woo her back to himself. In ch. 2, Yhwh's wife was the land. If we read the current verse in light of ch. 2, he brought his "wife" into the wilderness by creating a wilderness out of the land. The "children," that is, the people, would dwell in the land in tents, because the land became a wilderness, devoid of civilization. At that point, based on the continuation of ch. 2, the land would become fertile with the prosperity offered exclusively by Yhwh.

V. 11 Once Yhwh revealed Torah, the words of the prophets—placed there by Yhwh—ensured the people would follow his teaching. Speech and visions conveyed the teaching, which the people had to follow. Coming out of Egypt before, and coming out of corrupt Israel now, the people were filled with some other teaching inside them. Yhwh had to remove these aberrant words from them so only the words of Torah remained.

V. 12 This section plays on the Hebrew root גל, *gal*, "heap," to express how difficult the Israelites made it for Yhwh to provide them with prosperity. As discussed above in my remarks on 6:8 and ch. 5, Gilead represented fratricide, the epitome of disobedience. The people expressed their iniquity there through their warped justice.

Gilead further represented the pact made between two unfaithful, dishonest dealers, Jacob and Laban (Gen 31:47). Jacob put himself under Laban as a slave for fourteen years, worked to set up a situation where he could take possession of a large portion of Laban's sheep, and then snuck away in the night without a word to his host, father-in-law, and relative.[8] Laban tricked Jacob into squeezing him for slave labor, bargaining with his daughters. Jacob fled to גִּלְעָד, Gileʿad, to escape Laban, but Laban found him there. Once there, they made a pact by setting up a heap of stones as a testimony, which Jacob called in Hebrew, גַּלְעֵד, Galʿed, "heap (of) testimony." In Hebrew, "Gilead" and "Galʿed" are spelled with exactly the same consonants; only the vowels differ. The false players made an empty *galʿed* at *Gileʿad*.

The next location, Gilgal, linked the "heap" with the pattern of false worship to which Israel dedicated themselves. The consonants of גלגל, Gilgal, duplicate the Hebrew word, גל, gal, "heap," and share the root of "heap" with Gilead/Galʿed. They sacrificed to and worshiped their so-called god (maybe they even called it "Yhwh") at Gilgal.

The author played on these connections by using the root in its literal sense in the last strophe of the verse, showing that their behavior was like an obstacle in the way of a farmer. Farmers, even to our present day, understood that the beginning of the plowing season consists of removing stones from the field, so the plowing equipment can run smoothly. Heaps of stones cause hardship to the already difficult work of farming. Everything that Israel did to build up literal heaps of stones—altars and cities—as well as metaphorical ones—false agreements and apostasy—only made Yhwh's work more difficult. He would provide prosperity to the Israelites, but the "heaps" of injustice and falsehood make the work more difficult. Thus, their injustice came to cruelty, their pacts were false, and their worship distanced them from Yhwh.

---

[8] Laban was a relative of Rebeccah, Isaac's wife and Jacob's mother, and was therefore not a child of Abraham.

Vv. 13-14 I read these two verses together because they juxtapose the competing histories of Israel. Israel, the man, abandoned the land of his birthright in order to marry a woman, the son of Laban, so he made himself a slave to his uncle by occupying himself with raising Laban's sheep. Yhwh created the people, Israel, by bringing them out of slavery in Egypt by the hand of Moses, who kept them as his sheep. By contrasting the two agents, Jacob and Yhwh, Israel's god showed them how submission to Yhwh's freedom was superior to the Israel's self-determination that enslaved them.

V. 15 Yhwh would bring to Ephraim the natural consequence of their willfulness, upsetting Ephraim in the process. When the Assyrians invaded the Northern Kingdom, they would undermine the confidence of the people. The people would be left bloodied in the process—literally and figuratively.

Exodus history led to the promised land

The paternity test was in full swing. The people could follow in their father Jacob's rebellious, idolatrous, self-determined path, or in the path laid out by Yhwh. They were named after this rebellious one, hinting that this rebellion lay in their nature. Their choice of story lay before them.

Torah laid out a path to the land of milk and honey: follow Yhwh by the hand of Moses to end their slavery. Yhwh defeated their enemies, gave them food and drink in the מדבר, *midbar*, "wilderness," and imparted the words of wisdom at Sinai that would keep them on the right path.

Israel, however, followed the path of their rebellious forefather and namesake who left the land, enslaved himself, and fought against Yhwh. Ultimately, his nature set his family on a trajectory toward Egypt and the very enslavement from which Yhwh had to deliver them.

The people continued to act deceitfully, oppressing others for their gain. They believed themselves independent, but in fact enslaved themselves to their gods who demanded empty sacrifices, which they needed to extract from the weaker among them. Following their own plans for security left them vulnerable, without help from Yhwh.

Remembering the name and power of Yhwh, and his actions that glorified him, could give them hope. They could submit to the better way that Yhwh offered, instead of following their own will toward enslavement.

Chapter 13

¹When Ephraim spoke, he trembled; he lifted himself up in the midst of Israel, but he was ashamed by Baal and he died.

²And now they continue to sin, and they made for themselves an image from their silver and idols according to their understanding—the work of craftsmen all of it. They say to themselves, "Those who sacrifice a human, let them kiss calves."

³Therefore, they will be like a cloud of the morning and like the dew that goes away early; like chaff blown from the threshing floor and like smoke from the window.

⁴But I am Yhwh, your god from the land of Egypt, and a god besides me you do not know; there is no savior besides me.

⁵I, I knew you in the wilderness, in the land of heat.

⁶According to their pasture, they were satisfied, satisfied and their heart exalted; therefore, they forgot me.

⁷So I will be for them like a lion, like a leopard on the road to Assyria.

⁸I will meet them like a bereaved bear, and I will rend the enclosure of their heart, and I will devour them there like a lion—an animal of the field will tear them—

⁹Destroying you, O Israel, for it is by me, by your help.

¹⁰Where is your king? He will save you in all your cities. And your judges? whom you said, "Give me a king and princes"?

¹¹I give you a king in my anger and take him in my wrath.

¹²Bound up is the iniquity of Ephraim; hidden is his sin.

¹³The pangs of a woman giving birth are coming to him; he is a son who is not wise. Now he will not remain in the breeching of children.

¹⁴From the hand of Sheol I will ransom them; from death I will redeem them. I will be your plagues, O Death; I will be your destruction, O Sheol. Comfort will be hidden from my eyes.

¹⁵For he, a son of brothers, will bear fruit. An east wind will come; a wind of Yhwh from the wilderness will come up. His spring will dry, and his fount will be dried up. He shall spoil the treasury of every nice vessel.

¹⁶Samaria is ashamed because she rebelled against her god. By the sword they will fall, their infants shall be dashed to pieces, and their pregnant women will be torn open.[1]

Recent (attempted) fratricide

Yhwh emphasized his universal power as both provider and destroyer, and underscored the human impotence of the Northern Kingdom at stopping it. As we approach the end of the Book of Hosea, several themes are reprised here. Shame arising from adultery with other gods, as we saw in ch. 1, came upon Ephraim here, as they depended on the work of their hands to provide for and comfort them. Like their so-called love in ch. 6, the people themselves would evaporate like dew in ch. 13. Yhwh declared here his power from the beginning, in Egypt, as he did in ch. 12, and he will deprive them and destroy them, as he promised

---

[1] This verse is 14:1 in the Masoretic Text, although it ends with a section marker: a פ, or "*petuxah*."

in ch. 10 and was emotionally torn over in ch. 11. The kings, given to the people in their rebellion, would not help them, as described in ch. 8 and as they appeared to realize in ch. 9. Yet as the eagle foreshadowed in 8:1, their destruction was upon them. Instead of the idols alone being destroyed (8:6), or only the princes (7:16), all of the Northern Kingdom, including women and children, would be smashed.

We can read back into Hos 13 the story from 2 Kings about the Northern Kingdom's betrayal of their brother, Judah. While Hosea recalled Gibeah and the story of the Israelites' apostasy and fratricide against the Benjaminites, the same fratricide repeated itself with the approaching Assyrian threat against Samaria, as I explained in ch. 5. Ephraim habitually betrayed their brother and justified themselves. As a result, Yhwh would destroy the Northern Kingdom. Ephraim's move would bring on utter destruction, rather than protect their prosperity. Yhwh had to reveal his power to give life and to give death in order to deflate the proud heart of Ephraim. This process of betrayal and loss is summarized in the final verse.

Commentary

V. 1 The Northern Kingdom was the beginning and end of their problem. They decided to speak the word of Baal rather than the word of Yhwh, which led to their destruction. When Ephraim "lifted himself up" in the midst of Israel, this could refer to a specific event.

Since much of the Book of Hosea referred to the military conflicts between the North and the South, we can recall the episode when the Northern Kingdom and its allies rose up against the Southern Kingdom, preceding the Assyrian aggression (2 Kgs 16). In that episode, Ephraim exerted military pressure on Judah to ally themselves with the North against the encroaching Kingdom of Assyria.[2] Ephraim's pride led them not to faithfulness to Yhwh, but to self-reliance and self-congratulations as they followed Baal's teaching. No one looked good in the end except Yhwh. Rather than leading them to victory, Baal brought Ephraim to a shameful defeat.

V. 2 The religion of Ephraim fueled their self-righteousness by expiating their treachery effortlessly through an empty religious process. Armies brought home booty of silver and gold—possessions of those killed—when they returned victorious. As a gesture of thanks, they built an idol to their god, the one who brought them victory. They kissed the calf out of gratitude for their victory.

They did not give a thought, however, to the question of whether the war was faithful to Yhwh's teaching or not—and their idols do not argue. Idols cannot be stronger or wiser than the humans who created them, revealing any thanks to them to be foolish. Fortunately for the Ephraimites, the gods they chose over Yhwh required a trivially simple kiss of loyalty and did not condemn the sin of killing fellow human beings—even their own brothers to the South. Thus, the people used the looted goods for justifying the system that led to the death of their former owners.

V. 3 The people could not last by pledging fealty to objects with no power. The author described their loyalty with a metaphor of fleeting things: cloud, dew, chaff, and smoke. Previously in 6:4, Yhwh declared the people's love and loyalty as temporary as cloud and dew. All are here today, gone today—less

---

[2] In the end, Judah asked Assyria for assistance, so Assyria defeated and destroyed the Northern Kingdom, before turning and attacking Judah. Judah survived the attack by Yhwh's hand alone (2 Kgs 19:35).

than a day. The people would go the same way, along with their love. Their gods could not preserve them even for a moment.

V. 4 Yhwh declared the separation between himself and the other gods. Those idols never were not and never could be gods. When Israel was in Egypt and did not yet exist, Yhwh existed. No other god could create a people out of those who were not a people. Nations claimed other gods, and seduced Israel into believing in them, but they were not gods. They could not produce a people out of Torah. Yhwh alone could claim to be a god because of his power of salvation. To the same extent that Israel was temporary without him, Yhwh their god was as permanent as can be conceived.

V. 5 Even in the land of nothingness, the מדבר, *midbar*, "wilderness," Yhwh sustained Israel. Simply being known by Yhwh kept Israel alive, whereas the unmatched Egyptian army could not survive crossing the Red Sea. Yhwh knew the people he chose. He found them when they cried out in Egypt, and he kept them alive when they lived in a wilderness without food and water. He was a savior who brought them out of Pharaonic slavery and protected them once they were his. Had they stayed with this paradigm, they would not be in need, as they were at this moment in the story.

V. 6 Bounty spoiled the people.[3] Once they came out of the מדבר, *midbar*, "wilderness," they began to count on themselves. Yhwh freed and sustained them, yet they somehow felt that they could keep themselves going. Moreover, as they became more comfortable—"satisfied" is repeated twice in a row here in Hebrew—they became prouder and more self-sufficient. They

---

[3] Hosea already marked this tendency in 4:7 and 10:1.

forgot the one who gave birth to them and sustained their life as a people. They were doomed if they did not remember the only one who could protect them.

One of the three principle sins Yhwh listed in 4:1 is "knowledge of God," and the present verse showed how this absence looked: they forgot. Yhwh's gift of life, prosperity, and salvation, left their mind when they saw "their" possessions. Torah continuously teaches and reteaches what Yhwh did—even more than what Yhwh "is." When they forgot, Yhwh had to teach them again by removing his prosperity and protection, allowing the danger of wild animals and human enemies to afflict them.

V. 7 Because bounty spoiled them, Yhwh would have to take another tack. Instead of protecting the people from prey, Yhwh allowed threats like predatory felines to jump on and devour them. When Yhwh no longer protected them, he became the source of their danger. They needed adversity to recognize Yhwh's sovereignty as savior.

The immediacy of "the road to Assyria" is unclear. On the one hand, the *people* could be on the road to Assyria, in which case the people are heading to exile when they get attacked. One bad turn begets another. On the other hand, lions and leopards generally inhabited that highway, in which case *anyone* could get attacked in this area. In either case, Israel risked deadly attack when they did not depend on Yhwh.

V. 8 Yhwh's judgment came in the form of humans and beasts. All the forces of violence manifested Yhwh's judgment. Just as the Assyrians who came to exile Israel worked as the hand of Yhwh, more wild animals—bears, lions, and animals of the field—attacked them also, like in the previous verse.

The author played on the meaning of "heart" in this verse. In a literal sense, the bear will "rend" the chest cavity that holds the heart organ—a violent death. Metaphorically, the attack of the bear will tear apart the cavity that contains the *exalted*, smug thinking that Yhwh described in v. 6. Yhwh would destroy their pride. Their self-satisfied and self-reliant thinking made them forget Yhwh. Now nature's attack against them could kill them bodily and psychologically, by destroying any sense that the people could protect themselves.

V. 9   The same one who provided bounty as a savior destroyed them as a judge. Yhwh both helped in time of need and destroyed in time of judgment. He showed his power and strength by lifting up the weak who could not lift themselves up, and by destroying the powerful whom no other power could defeat. The "help" of Israel was Yhwh, who was currently destroying them.[4] Just as a

---

[4] This verse presents referential ambiguities as we try to understand who is doing what. The first phrase says literally "destroying you," followed by "Israel." Another clause follows, which literally says, "when/because by me by your help." Three questions thus arise. First, who or what is "destroying"? Second, what is the relationship between Yhwh (the "me" of "by me") and the help of Israel? Third, how does the destruction relate to the help?

For the first question, the first phrase focuses on the object of destruction, "you" (masculine singular), more than the agent of the destruction. I am reading "Yhwh" as the agent because this idea continues logically and syntactically from the previous verse. In this way, we can read from one verse to the next a continuous thought, "I will meet them like a bereaved bear . . . destroying you, O Israel. . . ." Yhwh emphasized that whether by means of a bear or other animal, he was the one destroying them, destroying "you."

"Israel" could, however, be the agent of the action, by which they were the cause of their own destruction, focusing on their disobedience as the root. Like the King James translation interpreted, "O Israel, thou hast destroyed thyself; but in me is thine help," Israel was destroying itself, while Yhwh was their help. The previous two verses, however, defined Yhwh's role as the director of their destruction, making the point that he is the lion, leopard, and bear. Their role has passed, back when they decided to trust their king. Yhwh was now destroying them.

child seeks comfort from the same parent who punished him, Yhwh was the only functioning power. No matter what violence one faces, it comes from the same figure who brings relief. The people could not overcome the destruction that came to them without rebelling against the one who sent it. At the same time, the only path to safety was following the teaching that Yhwh provided and they transgressed. This interpretation flows from the recent verses and chapters, which emphasized that he was their god *since Egypt*. He already showed his beneficence when he brought the people out of Pharaonic slavery and into his service, as he cared for them in the wilderness. Life when there was no prosperity came from the same source as destruction when there was a bounty. Yhwh remained the source of both.

V. 10 The king looked small once Yhwh showed himself to be the god in control of all the forces at play in the life of Israel. Even though they ostensibly admitted the impotence of their king in 10:3, he mocked their admission here. The king could not do anything in the face of such power. The people wanted a king and princes, thinking that they held some power, especially military power. Assyria's attack proved the worthlessness of this belief, of

---

For the second question, the author ironically juxtaposed Yhwh, the source of destruction, with Yhwh, the source of help. As he saved Israel, he destroyed Pharaoh. He could destroy Israel just as easily, but also save them via Torah. Such juxtaposition can be uncomfortable if one does not like the idea of Yhwh as the cause of Israel's destruction. One could feasibly translate not "by me" but "against me," so that the phrase reads, ". . . because they [Israel] are against me. . . ." This interpretation can make sense because the destruction transpired because of their rebellion against him. Nevertheless, they were destroyed by Yhwh, the judge and punisher, even if their end appeared to come through wild animal attack.

The answers to the first and second questions lead to the answer of the third question, that Yhwh presented himself as the only deity of the people. Yhwh destroyed them to make a point, not due to sadism. The reason for Yhwh to destroy Israel was to show that he was their only help. By overpowering any hope they had in saving themselves, he alone remained in their mind.

their misplaced trust. Not only was their king powerless against the Assyrians, but so was any defense that confronted the invincible power of Yhwh.

V. 11 Yhwh never supported their king, and he could remove him at his pleasure. Granting a king reminds the reader of 1 Sam 8, where Yhwh allowed the people one as a sign of their rejecting him and his rule. This request, moreover, sounds suspiciously similar to their request in the previous verse (Hos 13:10). Yhwh then eliminated the king during the invasion of the Assyrians.

Furthermore, Yhwh asserted that the king was not only powerless by himself, but whatever power he might possess came from Yhwh; the king served at his pleasure. Since Yhwh claimed the violence of the invasion, he argued here that a king whom Yhwh put in place could not divert a threat from the same power. The people could not play one power against another, because only one power existed.

V. 12 Iniquity, rebellion from Yhwh, resulted inevitably in negative consequences, because the people turned from their source of life and protection. Hence, the iniquity is "bound up" and "hidden" or "stored up" with its consequences.[5] We imagine the litany of incorrect actions of Ephraim—faith in a king, self-serving religious practices, neglect of the weak—lying in a storehouse alongside the consequences about to be unloaded on Ephraim. Soon, the sin would be revealed in its consequences.

V. 13 The moment of birth is coming, but whose son would he be? This question returns from the beginning of the book. They would not pass the paternity test that would show Yhwh to be their father because their lack of wisdom would become apparent.

---

[5] The root צרר, *tsarar*, can mean both "hide" and "store up."

The consequences of their actions were imminent and inevitable, just as a mother knows when the time comes to give birth. Ephraim was the son who caused pain to his mother. He performed foolish actions because he did not understand the inevitability of consequences. In modern discussion, we would call this "immaturity." The children would be destroyed in the inevitable, upcoming war.

V. 14 Grammatically, two entities could potentially be desiring "comfort" in the last clause: Sheol/Death and the people. Sheol/Death is the closest antecedent in the text, as the threat of destruction came against them in this verse. Nevertheless, a similar threat in the previous verse came against the people. Yhwh remained steadfast and would not change his mind, however. In a single power move, Yhwh would prove to the people that only he controlled death by bringing destruction to them, and in the process would prove that Sheol does nothing on its own without Yhwh giving him the ability to do so. As Israel saw, Yhwh is not necessarily omnibenevolent, as they received no comfort when he killed their brothers and sisters. At the same time, Sheol/Death could not even be comforted by their own power. Everyone would be forced to concede that Yhwh alone was omnipotent.

When Yhwh worked to bring Israel back under his aegis, he had to show his superlative strength against both the people and the so-called power of Death and Sheol. In spite of imminent destruction, Yhwh could still save them from death. A transaction would transfer possession of the people to Yhwh from the complete destruction they bound themselves to. This action reflected the shift in Exodus, when the people went from under Pharaoh's aegis to Yhwh's. Whereas the latter took them out of Egypt previously, now he would take them out of Sheol, the land of the dead, and away from Death itself. As he destroyed the might of Egypt in the process of the Exodus, Sheol and its power would also be upended; death would no longer have power over Yhwh's people.

Yhwh's omnipotence encompassed even the power of death. If Yhwh had the power of life, he also wielded death. No ability lay outside of Yhwh's purview. As Baal did not have the power to give life, so Sheol did not have the power to mete out death.

V. 15 As the manifestation of Yhwh's wrath came to the people, all prosperity would disappear. When Israel enjoyed prosperity and their work bore fruit, Yhwh thwarted them by sending an "east wind." The latter bears a double meaning. The literal east wind is dry and will damage crops, a "wind of Yhwh" from the desert. It will ruin their agricultural prosperity. When we understand the east wind metaphorically, it represents Assyria, a similarly destructive force from the East. That army would come to steal their material prosperity as booty. As a result, this wind would dry up their water supplies and spoil their treasury.

Similarly, the "wind of Yhwh" bears a double-meaning. First, the wind of destruction across the Jordanian desert would be coming to carry out Yhwh's will by the hand of the Assyrians. Second, רוח, *rûax*, can mean "wind" or "spirit." When we hear that the "spirit of Yhwh will come from the wilderness (מדבר, *midbar*)," the mention of the desert triggers our mind to recall the Exodus and the Revelation at Sinai. That spirit was Torah, Yhwh's teaching. Thus, this strike that Assyria would effect against Israel would come as the realization of Torah.

V. 16 This verse begins the conclusion to the first phase of the Book of the Twelve. Samaria betrayed the source of their prosperity and so were devastated. While the reader was struck by the gore of dashed infants and torn-open pregnant women, the image worked on a level deeper than the naked gore. The next generation would be annihilated. With this destruction would come the end of any future hope of Samaria.

We began in Hos 1 with the betrayal of the land and the repercussions, and now in the upcoming ch. 14, the author focused on the betrayal of Samaria and the death manifested in their land. In the first chapters of the book their rebellion was described as זנונים, *zenûnîm*, "harlotries" against a husband, and now the verb is מרה, *marâ*, "rebel" against their god.

End of self-reliance

The author capped off these thirteen chapters with a summary of the relationship between Israel and Yhwh up to this point. Ephraim planned to defend itself from Assyria. The fear of Assyrian invasion caused them to abandon Yhwh's teaching by turning to foreign gods and governments, and against their fellow-Israelites, Judah. Although such an attack against their own people revealed their sin, they worked out a religious system to expunge their guilt. Thus, they could betray Yhwh's Torah with impunity and feel good about it.

They were impossible students. Their willful insistence on their own terms deadened any ability to learn Torah: the imperative to serve their brother and sister and accept adversity from Yhwh's hand. Their heart grew proud and full of itself. Yhwh had to plan for how he would open it.

The solution would need to confront the deep sickness and hard-headedness at the core of Ephraim. Yhwh sent an enemy that Ephraim could not defeat. Their destruction and the end of their prosperity—in spite of their military allies and religious cult—

would prove that Yhwh alone controlled the forces of prosperity. He would bring destruction to death itself. Only he granted life and death.

Reversing course required that the next generation accept defeat from Assyria as a judgment from Yhwh, and display charity toward their brother, Judah. Should they do so, Ephraim would prove that they finally understood. Yhwh continued to confront the demonstrated inability of Israel to follow his law, yet he did not relent in teaching them. Since the bounty Yhwh offered them had already spoiled them, only a generation born of Yhwh would turn back to Torah by feeling the awful sting of judgment.

Chapter 14

¹*Return, O Israel, to Yhwh your god, because you have stumbled in your sin.*¹

²*Take with you words and return to Yhwh; say to him,*² *"Bear all iniquity and accept good, and let us render calves with our lips.*³

³*"Assyria will not save us. On a horse we will not ride. We will no longer say, 'Our god!' to the works of our hands, O you in whom the orphan finds mercy."*

⁴*I will heal their apostasy, I will love them voluntarily, for my anger has turned away from them.*

---

¹ This verse is 14:2 in Hebrew. Israel is addressed here with a singular masculine pronoun.
² This and all the preceding verbs of this verse use the plural from of address.
³ This last phrase *with our lips* requires explanation. Many translators render this phrase as "the fruit of our lips" (NIV, NASB, ISV). This reading cannot arise directly from the Hebrew for two reasons. First, Hebrew פרים, *parîm*, most likely means "calves" from the singular פר, *par*. It is less likely that comes from פרי, *parî*, "fruit," because the word here appears in an unusual form; this noun rarely appears with a plural ending. Second, the normal way of expressing the genitive in Hebrew would be with a construct state, which we do not see, since this form פרים, *parîm*, cannot be a construct state.

I translated this phrase with a preposition, even though the preposition does not appear in Hebrew, because it is less of a difficulty and because it solves the problem that the Israelites could not previously overcome. I have translated the bare noun here as "with our lips." Biblical Hebrew, like English, expresses the instrumental role that the lips would play with a preposition, -ב, *b-*. It is also common in Biblical Hebrew, though, to indicate an instrumental role with a bare noun, without a preposition, as I have translated. (This usage is called "means/method" in Christo H. J van der Merwe, Jackie A Naudé, and Jan H Kroeze, *A Biblical Hebrew Reference Grammar* [Sheffield: Sheffield Academic Press, 1999], §33.3(ii); and "non-cognate internal accusative" in Bruce Waltke and Michael O'Connor, *An Introduction to Biblical Hebrew Syntax* [Winona Lake, IN: Eisenbrauns, 1990], §10.2.1g.)

⁵*I will be like dew for Israel. He will grow like the lily. He will stretch out his roots like the Lebanon.*

⁶*His branches will go out; and his beauty will be like the olive tree and his smell like the Lebanon.*

⁷*Those dwelling in his shade will turn, they will give life to the grain, and they will grow like the vine, his memory like the wine of Lebanon.*

⁸*Ephraim: "What have idols to do with me anymore?" I answered and beheld him, "I am like a flourishing cypress tree. From me your fruit is found."*

⁹*Who is wise will understand these things; the understanding will know them. For straight are the ways of Yhwh, and righteous ones walk in them, and the transgressors stumble in them.*

Repeat after me . . .

The attack of the Assyrians was the judgment against Israel, and Yhwh showed his mercy by "feeding" Ephraim in this final chapter the lines he had to say and do to be declared righteous. Up to this point, Yhwh showed how Israel failed to live correctly by their teachings, words, and actions; in ch. 14, though, he told them what they should have been saying all along. The actions and threats of the preceding chapters ought to have impressed upon the people the correct actions and words to embody. They needed to follow none other than Yhwh as their king and god.

Yhwh then described the life that they would have, should they follow these words. Life would be good: fruitful and prosperous. Sadly, the people possessed the tools for speaking and acting correctly before this point, yet they did not take advantage of them. Their opportunity passed, but it remained for the next generation.

Those who caused this judgment would not be able to change in time before their doom arrived, so the hope would rest in the next generations. Those who hear the words of this book will know what was said and done to bring this destruction, and now will bear the burden of knowing how to speak and act correctly for hope to remain in Israel. The paternity test does not apply only to the first generation but to every future offspring of the land.

This chapter raises some confusion in Hebrew because of the multiple ways Israel is referenced. At the end of the previous chapter (13:16), Samaria was a rebellious woman. This depiction hearkened back to the image of Yhwh's bride in the beginning of Hosea. The prophet addressed Israel directly as a single man (14:1), and as a group of people who responded as a collective "we" (in 14:2-3).[4] We can understand Israel, therefore, as a collective entity who had to make a series of individual choices if they wanted to obey and trust in Yhwh as their collective deity.

This chapter addressed itself to its readership in a more direct way than the rest of the book. Whereas the rest of the book speaks to Israel, who caused the Assyrian invasion, this chapter addresses the present reader, in the generation that followed the invasion. The earlier generation got no more chances; the consequences were locked in. Historically speaking, we know that Assyria invaded and devastated this part of the world. Yet in 14:1, Israel is asked to "return; repent," and in v. 9, the final verse of this chapter (and of the book), "the wise" who listen and act on the

---

[4] "The people of Israel" can similarly be both singular and plural in English, that is, "The people of Israel *is*..." and "The people of Israel *are*..." are both grammatical.

words of this book are addressed. The next generation can benefit and prosper. The chapter offers the book as a משל, *mashal*, "parable" for the listener—the next generation—to learn from and act on.

Commentary

V. 1 Hosea presented over the course of thirteen chapters the case for Israel's deep self-reliance as the source of their problems; here he offered another chance for the addressee, Israel, to repent. The identity of "Israel" in this verse is twofold. On the one hand, the audience inside the story heard this and, even though they faced the consequences of their sin as the Assyrian invasion threatened, the prophet exhorted them to accept the consequences that were coming because Yhwh sent them. They sinned and could now embrace the consequences as a way to learn and be wise.

On the other hand, the audience of later generations who hears the text in their present can take the "stumble" as a past event they can potentially recover from. The Israel who listens to the written text now can take the example of their forefathers as how *not* to act and speak. By noting how their fathers stumbled, and how Yhwh reacted, the hearer of the text can learn and act in a wiser fashion. The following verses give them the recipe for success.[5]

V. 2 Israel must prostrate itself at Yhwh's feet, admitting their inability to do the right thing. The prophet told the people what words to pronounce toward Yhwh.

---

[5] I began ch. 14 with this verse, against the Hebrew chapter numbering, because the Hebrew text marked the end of 14:1 with a section marker (called a "*petuxah*") and because the previous verse fit more with the theme of destruction in ch. 13. This theme is not found in ch. 14.

Chapter 14

The type of calves Israel offered previously—sacrificial calves—have, at best, not helped and, at worst, undermined any good they wanted to do. Yhwh commanded them to stop the sacrificing, and the prophet here commanded them to speak correctly. As a result, the people needed to replace their useless sacrifices with the correct words, and then do with their words—their "lips"—what they were trying to do with their calves. Their lips would thus perform the role the calves were supposed to, that is, profess the people's fidelity and obedience to Yhwh.

The author made the people pronounce the correct words:

Bear all iniquity, because they have to admit that they constantly rebel, that it is a sickness they bear chronically.

Accept good, because on occasion they do the right thing, even if they may undermine it in the next breath or action.

Let us render calves with our lips, since they know that actual sacrifice leads them astray. Furthermore, may Yhwh value these vows from their mouths, that he might assume that imminent action will manifest the vows.

V. 3 Israel had to denounce the false powers in their lives and to express true fealty to their god. They were mutually exclusive. Military power and idols could not save them. Significantly, they did not simply dedicate themselves to the deity with supreme power, but the one who used this power to protect the weak. Yhwh was the functional father to the person without paternal oversight. Strength would not help Israel, except to strengthen the weakest. This epithet, the one who shows mercy to orphans, reminded Israel that Yhwh would help them when they were weak; they did not need strength from other sources.

V. 4 Yhwh decided to treat the people as he saw fit, in spite of what they deserved based on their past words and actions. While they may or may not have pronounced the appropriate words cited in the last two verses, he could choose to consider them faithful. The word "heal" zeroes in on the deep nature of the people's unfaithfulness as a sickness. He could heal their turning away from him by *choosing* to love them. No matter their words or even actions, they could not coerce or force him to treat them in a particular way. Once he decided to redirect or turn off his anger—which referred to his wrathful actions, not an emotion—he no longer imposed on the people the situations they had been suffering from. He could turn on the prosperity again at his pleasure.

Vv. 5-7 The people would grow and prosper with Yhwh as their source. Previously, the prophet depicted the people's love as "dew," which disappeared with the heat of the sun (Hos 6:4), and the people themselves as passing "dew," like the chaff of the threshing floor, that would pass away (Hos 13:3). When Yhwh is depicted as dew here, it represented lushness and prosperity. He caused the growth of his garden, Israel.

In a scene reminiscent of Ps 1, Israel would grow with the prosperity provided by Yhwh when they follow Torah. Furthermore, others would live in the protection, the "shade," of Yhwh as Israel manifested Torah. That is, Gentiles would live alongside Israel, benefitting from the grace given to the latter as a result of their fidelity to Yhwh's instruction. Once they became faithful, they would correctly understand that the grain and wine—believed to come from Baal in chs. 1 and 2—came from Yhwh. As the people enjoyed the fruits of the vine, the "memory" of Yhwh and his faithfulness to them would grow, not only among Israel, but among all those who would dwell in their shade.

Significantly, all three verses employ a simile with "Lebanon," a beautiful, prosperous region on the edge of the territory of the twelve tribes.[6] If Israel would turn back to Yhwh, he could provide for them abundantly, even if at or beyond the edge of what they considered "their" territory. The length of his reach could comfort even those in faraway exile in Assyria.[7]

V. 8 The content of the Book of Hosea ends with Ephraim speaking correctly and Yhwh responding with gracious generosity. Not idols but Yhwh provided prosperity—the thesis this book began with. When the people accepted prosperity from him, they continued to receive what they needed. The good works of Yhwh toward them would produce, in this way, good works from the people, because the people would respond with trust (faith) rather than employ disloyal idolatry to hedge their bets. The people could act correctly thanks to the grace of Yhwh. When Yhwh offered love and an end of wrath in v. 4, the people began to flourish again, manifested in actions consistent with Yhwh's teaching. Grace would provide the opportunity to act graciously.

The garden of Eden would function again. Yhwh would be the cypress tree, and Israel's fruit would come from him. Once the people would realize that idolatry provided them nothing, that only Yhwh provided for them, they would benefit from Yhwh's fruit. They would cultivate and so eat from the garden Yhwh arranged for them. Yhwh would provide for all the people's needs, as they ate the fruit and obeyed. Following any other teaching, any other deity, would end their access to the prosperity of the garden.

---

[6] In Deut 11:24, "the Lebanon" is paired with המדבר, *hammidbar*, "the wilderness," as geographic edges of the territory of the Israelites.

[7] The reach of Yhwh's arm became clear in Ezekiel, as he appeared in Babylon, riding his heavenly chariot.

V. 9 The final words of the book interpret the entire preceding text of the book, "these things," as a משל, *mashal*, "parable," for the reader to learn from. Having finished hearing the Book of Hosea, the reader can now become wise. These words challenge the reader/hearer of the book. If one understands them, he or she is wise; if not, he or she is not wise.

The paternity test was clear. If one is obedient to Yhwh as to a father, one is walking in the right ways; if one is disobedient, one is not walking in them. The book already sufficed to determine who was wise and righteous, based on one's actual understanding and performance of what the text commands. The test was simple. One must be wary of the consequences.

These final words pointed to the correct "script," cited in this chapter, that Yhwh offered to put in their mouths. The hearer must strive for wisdom and knowledge so that he or she can understand the key words of the book. As explained multiple times in the preceding chapters, putting aside trust in any power—a military or another deity—leads the reader on the path of wisdom. One must possess the wisdom to desire to seek wisdom.

Words of life

This chapter offers the correct words for the people within the story to reflect the correct attitude toward Yhwh, presenting the whole book as a משל, *mashal*, "parable," to the reader of the story. If the people's actions had remained consistent to these words, their problems would have ended. On their own, the people did not have the power to resist drought or invasion, and they likewise did not have that power with Baal's or their army's intervention. They already stumbled; now they can walk straight while protected by Yhwh.

By following Yhwh, the people—if not the present, doomed generation, then perhaps future ones who would read this text—would prosper. They would no longer expend resources on armies or sacrifices, but instead on the poor in their community. The rich would no longer need to depend on their ability to hoard; the entire people could benefit from wealth.

Most importantly, if they obeyed, Yhwh would no longer need to remind them of his power by imposing deprivation on them. Since ch. 1, Yhwh had been pulling away from the people, showing them that without his power, they withered. Now Yhwh promised to be "dew" so that Israel could "grow" and "stretch out roots."

Wisdom and knowledge lay at the root of correct action. Pursuing them would have healed their deep sickness of rebellion. The words allow the hearer to understand the message, even when the hearer is sick and wants to believe in any other power besides Yhwh. The message also contains the cure: complete submission to the power of Yhwh.

Conclusions

Freedom for the next generation

Baal is not only the ancient god of a long-extinct civilization. Baal-worship is not primitive or distant. His cult is celebrated today, throughout humanity at every military parade, at the dedication of every new skyscraper and mall, from the towers of Washington, DC, and Beijing, to the American Midwest and the jungles of Indonesia. In a most cunning fashion, we find him triumphant in university laboratories and even in houses of worship that ironically bear the name of Yhwh, Lord.

Yhwh sought three things: faithfulness, kindness, and knowledge of god. He did not find them before, and he cannot find them today. Hosea thus shouts across the generations, from the first worshipers of Baal to today's. Yhwh is searching; what will he find?

The call is simple, only three desires that would manifest Yhwh's holiness. The prophet offers freedom through simplification. Give up the institutions that enslave you. Simply leave them behind. Grasp the divine knowledge of Yhwh's word, Torah, remain faithful to it, and perform acts of חסד, *xesed*, "kindness."

Instead of the virtues that Yhwh seeks, we pursue the opposite: dedication to oneself, withholding kindness, and the rejection of wisdom. Humans gladly submit to and follow their Baal-infested heart, which compels them to build up and preserve themselves.

So that the next generation might live free of Baal to serve Yhwh alone, we are duty-bound to learn Torah and teach it to them. Our eyes see clearly that our current generation cannot hold fast to the word of Yhwh, always seeking to return to the slavery of

Egypt, even if they find themselves in Detroit, Duesseldorf, or Delhi. This generation has no hope, so we must look to the next. Hosea does not bring hope to the listener, but the duty to give hope to those yet unborn.

Faithfulness and the original betrayal

The world around us is essentially good and beautiful, thanks to Yhwh's provision. In the beginning, Yhwh took an empty land, "married" it, and filled it with life. Hosea referred to the Exodus as the moment when the land gave "birth" to the people. The barren desert of Sinai brought forth and sustained an entire nation, thanks to the seed and provision of Yhwh.

Whoredom sadly ruined this idyll. The land-wife thought that each deity provided his own thing as he was able. More relationships with more "boyfriends" hedged her bets and provided more safety and comfort, just in case Yhwh or another god did not provide. She chose elusory security over loyalty to the one who gave her life and beauty.

Now that she betrayed him, it was time for Yhwh to repeat his courtship. He would reduce her to desert once again to fill her up anew with life. The broken relationship between husband and wife, god and land, began the drama that unfolded in Hosea.

With such a promiscuous mother, the paternity of the children is in question. The children of the land must trust completely in Yhwh's provision, and turn their backs on their mother's lovers, to prove that they were his children.

Like them, our paternity is up for debate. Will the hearer of Hosea show his or her faithfulness? The answer, sadly, is "no."

Conclusions

חסד, xesed, and idolatry

Yhwh represents the force beyond human pursuits, the one who controls all the forces of life and death that Baal cannot. In every generation, he provides food, health, psychological well-being, and safety—on his terms, not ours. Humans court the forces that feel good, and avoid those that hurt, but Yhwh employs both for his purposes. Every generation knows very well that human powers of manipulation are limited; Hosea defined what lies beyond that limit as "Yhwh."

The ancients built temples to house their statues of bronze. (Whether their mouths dedicated them to Baal or Yhwh is not important.) Modern humans cannot stop building images devoted to their efforts and institutions that bring them prosperity and freedom, from the Euro statue at the Willi-Brandt-Platz in Frankfurt to the Statue of Liberty in New York Harbor. Ancient priests and modern economists dedicated to the ideals depicted in these works promised to keep us safe from the forces beyond our control.

Idols require more silver and gold, which enrich some and impoverish others. Lawmakers take away people's liberty—though never their own—for the sake of "security." Homeless people sleep across the street from the Euro statue in Frankfurt thanks to "economic prosperity." Humans' best efforts are ineffective, at best, but most consistently, cruel.

Even in Hosea's day, people defined idolatry too narrowly. "Idolatry" does not exclusively refer to "kissing calves."[1] Hosea 5 related Mizpah to idolatry, not because of a cultic action, but because they turned the commandments of Yhwh on their head.

---

[1] This reference comes from 13:2.

Justice turned to genocide, and they chose to believe in a military leader for safety. Their faith in Baalism and their own justice drove a wedge between themselves and their savior, Yhwh.

These were not one-time decisions, though, but a deep sickness in every member of humanity (Hos 6). Every human being naturally believes that warring against injustice is a moral good, even if some innocents are hurt along the way. Scripture, though, declared it apostasy because one no longer counted on Yhwh and his Torah for safety and justice, and because it assumed the human justice-seeker to be just—a trait that could only be ascribed to Yhwh. Further making the point, harming innocents could not be just, undermining the very fight. Greed rendered obedience impossible. Yhwh promised to offer what the people needed, but for some this did not suffice. They relied on themselves to take more than their portion, resulting in shortages. Poverty was created by greed. Israel showed themselves consistently unreliable (Hos 7).

Just like their ancestors felt after leaving Egypt, readers of every generation find themselves under Yhwh while longing for Pharaoh and other gods. For illusory safety humans enslave themselves to a king and idols through fortresses and rituals (Hos 8). When their own king appears inadequate, they look for another one, like the ruler of Assyria or the next president. Yet, neither can deliver the safety they promise. Furthermore, both kings and Baals constantly require more wealth—whether via taxes or sacrifices—from the people, yet can never be satisfied. In spite of Torah, people forget that their substance comes from Yhwh.

חסד, *xesed*, flows when we turn from the false powers that keep us safe and comfortable. We no longer block the flow of prosperity to others or take more than our share. To the measure that Yhwh has provided for us, we offer provision to others—not as our surplus, but as what Yhwh possesses and offers to anyone in need.

Once we reject faithfulness to Yhwh, kindness ceases, but when we quit our Baals and pursue Yhwh, we begin to show mercy to others. We stop creating institutions that should protect us, but in fact exploit others. We set aside the terror of insecurity for acceptance of the good and evil, life and death, that inevitably come to us. Free of fear, we can perform acts of חסד, *xesed*.

Choosing Torah, the knowledge of god

Scripture used the relationship of father and son as a metaphor for teacher and student. A teacher begets a student through teaching, and the student becomes the "son" of the teacher. That student, however, may reject his paternity by rejecting the teaching offered to him.

Who is Israel's father, then? Yhwh begot them not when they entered the land but in Sinai, specifically when he taught them Torah, the knowledge of god that required loyalty and mercy, and provided for rich and poor alike. Soon after, however, they discovered the teaching of Baal, which required sacrifices, temple worship, and military strength for the sake of national and individual prosperity. The people chose the latter, the teaching of Baal, and rejected Yhwh as their father.

The Book of Hosea presented Yhwh's method of laying the groundwork anew so that future generations might prosper. Yhwh first laid Israel to waste to prepare for a new exodus in which he could beget the next generation, so that they might be loyal to his teaching. The destruction and lambasting preached by the prophet drilled to the diseased heart of the human mind so that Torah might heal it.

Religion corrupts justice and excludes mercy; it rejects Torah. The mechanism of human faithlessness follows a pattern. It begins when the priests become masters of ritual and forget their charge of teaching the people obedience to Torah, and so withhold Yhwh's instruction for their own gain (Hos 4). When the link between the teaching and the people breaks, no hope for obedience remains—only sin. Filling the vacuum left by Torah, the priests teach cheap religion. Follow a few arbitrary rules to remain "in," and if you mess up, give a portion of your wealth to the priests. Kiss a calf—your sin will be forgiven. Wisdom is forsaken.

A future hope

Hosea's audience is thus invited to accept Torah, reject the teaching they learned to follow from their forefathers, and become loyal sons and daughters of Yhwh. Rather than fear the forces that hurt us, we can embrace them as coming from the author of life. Instead of sustaining damage, the forces of "evil" that Yhwh employs will teach us our own helplessness and dependence on Yhwh, shattering our Baals.

Yhwh required no empty gesture from his hearers except truth, kindness, and divine knowledge (Hos 4:1). For Yhwh to prove that people must trust him alone, he showed that he controlled their substance and livelihood. Hence, he held back their sustenance and stopped defending them, so they could see with their own eyes the uselessness of their idols and fortresses (Hos 10).

Every generation must choose slavery or freedom, obedience to Baal and king or to Yhwh. Israel has two patrimonies. The first was their namesake, Jacob-Israel, evident through their struggle against their brother and God. The second was from Moses, which offered them Torah (Hos 12). Whenever people are enslaved, exodus is possible—even from Assyria—by Yhwh's mercy and powerful, outstretched arm (Hos 11).

Yhwh had to break people's hearts open to cure the deep disease of faithlessness (Hos 13). They did not understand because their religion expunged their guilt, leaving no trace that the people may have disobeyed Torah. If they did not see that they disobeyed, there was no hope. Nevertheless, Hosea placed in front of his hearers a book, *his* book. Should we listen to it and learn from the sin of the last generation, we can have hope for wisdom and life by following the words of Torah, and shunning idolatry and military power (Hos 14).

These words close Hosea but open the rest of the Book of the Twelve. Now when one continues further into the Book of the Twelve, the main themes and definitions are clear. "Idolatry" means depending on any power besides Yhwh's and believing that good—or bad—comes from a power other than that deity. Militarism, a subset of idolatry, depends on an army for safety. Religious practices imply that performing particular actions will selfishly help me; such is also idolatry. Through the rest of the Book of the Twelve, idolatry is the stick to measure the people's disloyalty against their god.

Our generation does not differ from Hosea's. We, like them, set up governments and religions that make us feel safe, which, in turn, require resources to save us at the expense of the poor. We have to count on ourselves, and the kings and gods we created. We continue to take more for ourselves and more from the poor, in order to perpetuate a regime that cannot help us.

Likewise, we have not filled our world with truth, חסד, *xesed*, or knowledge of God. Torah is dangerous to our independent self-interest. Even though more of us are college educated than ever in history, we would rather read quotes and memes from the Bible than read the word of Yhwh for ourselves. Our religions focus on who is in and who is out, rather than opening Yhwh's word for all to hear. Too much mercy puts us at risk. If we submitted to our enemies, offered up our prosperity to the poor, and took no more than we needed for the day, we could never imagine that we were safe.

We are enslaved, while, tragically, the freedom of Torah lies right at our fingertips.

The only hope is the next generation. We can teach them today. We can tell them what justice looks like, what mercy looks like, and—more importantly than anything—what Torah teaches. They may enjoy emancipation from the institutions we bore them into, no longer our sons and daughters, but children of Yhwh. He may free them in the next exodus, offering them Torah once again, in the hope of the obedience that eluded our grasp.

May Yhwh recognize them as his children.

www.ingramcontent.com/pod-product-compliance
Lightning Source LLC
Chambersburg PA
CBHW051041160426
43193CB00010B/1023